THE *Field Guide* TO
CATTLE

THE *Field Guide* TO
CATTLE

By Valerie Porter
Photography by Lynn M. Stone

Voyageur Press

First published in 2008 by Voyageur Press, an imprint of MBI Publishing Company,
Galtier Plaza, Suite 200, 380 Jackson Street, St. Paul, MN 55101 USA

Voyageur Press titles are also available at discounts in bulk quantity for industrial or sales-
promotional use. For details write to Special Sales Manager at MBI Publishing Company,
Galtier Plaza, Suite 200, 380 Jackson Street, St. Paul, MN 55101 USA.

To find out more about our books, join us online at www.voyageurpress.com.

Library of Congress Cataloging-in-Publication Data
Porter, Valerie, 1942-
  The field guide to cattle / by Valerie Porter ; photography by Lynn M. Stone.
      p. cm.
  Includes bibliographical references and index.
  ISBN-13: 978-0-7603-3192-7 (plc)
  ISBN-10: 0-7603-3192-8 (plc)
  1. Cattle—United States. 2. Cattle breeds—United States. 3. Cattle—Behavior. I. Stone, Lynn
M. II. Title.
SF197.P67 2008
636.2—dc22   2007021848

On the half title page: A Holstein cow.
On the title page, left: Swiss Brown cows in their native Alpine setting. **Right:** A Pinzgauer cow.
Opposite: Typically shaggy White Galloway cows.
On the contents page: A pleasantly mature Hereford cow.

Edited by Danielle J. Ibister
Designed by LeAnn Kuhlmann

The cattle names Panda®, Belted Irish Jersey®, Belted Milking Dexter®, American Beltie®,
Mini Holstein®, Barbee®, and Five Breed Grad-Wohl® are trademarks owned by Professor
Emeritus Richard Gradwohl and are used here by permission.

Printed in China

Dedication

To Rosie, a much-loved and loving Jersey house cow, who taught me to slow down.

Acknowledgments

I am forever in debt to the late Ian L. Mason, who died at the age of ninety-three in May 2007 and who worked for many years with the UN's FAO in Rome, traveling the world to discover more about livestock. He opened my eyes to the huge number of breeds all over the world and generously invited me to edit the fifth edition of his authoritative World Dictionary on livestock breeds, types, and varieties when, in his late eighties, he finally decided he was a little too old to continue this lifelong project.

I am also grateful to Lynn Stone for his magnificent photographs of the breeds in this book.

Contents

Introduction

The Pleasure of Cows

The essence of cows is their warmth, generosity, stolidity, and sense of peaceful contemplation. They often have a dreamy faraway look in their eyes as they chew their cud or suckle a calf. For the hand-milker there can be a great feeling of mutual companionship when you squat on a three-legged stool with your forehead pressed against a cow's flank while your hands rhythmically extract milk from her capacious udder and the streams of warm, frothing creamy liquid squirt into the pail. But very few cows are milked by hand nowadays; most dairy cows live in large, impersonal commercial herds where they are milked by machine. Another large group of cows function as sucklers, rearing their own calves for the beef market. An even larger group includes animals destined for the plate—steers and heifers (young cows) fattened for the slaughterhouse, whether raised on milk and grass or in huge feedlots. At heart, they are all bovines and can all be seen as individuals if you have the time and patience to understand and respect them.

Jersey cows are near neighbors of the Guernsey in the Channel Islands. The Jersey's dished face is a useful aid to identification.

Opposite: A Guernsey cow meets temptation. Most cows enjoy crunching on apples.

The handsome pied pattern of a Holstein cow's coat has always been a favorite among dairy farmers.

How to approach a cow

The best way to approach a cow is to be still and let the cow come to you. If you watch quietly, cows will often come over out of curiosity. They may be wary, so be patient.

- Exude an air of calm and relaxation.
- Talk quietly (if at all).
- Keep any movements to a minimum and always slow. Do nothing sudden.
- Let the animal sniff you. She might lick your hand (this is an honor) with her very rough tongue, or she might lick your jacket or footwear.

If you reach out your hand, you will cause alarm. The cow will pull back. Cattle are prey animals in the wild, and you are a potential predator. The cow's eye is designed to be aware of approaching predators, and an approaching hand looms large.

If you meet a herd of cows with calves, expect the mothers to be protective of their young; if a dog accompanies you, they can become aggressive. Steers or young heifers will probably be skittish in the open and seem to chase you, but it's generally mischief and curiosity, not aggression (unless you have that dog), and if you stand your ground, they'll skid to a halt. A flap of the arms and shouting might make them back off, but they will continue to follow you across the field. When you leave, walk, don't run. To make them hightail it away, try imitating the buzz of a gadfly or the hiss of an aerosol spray can.

Beware of the bull!

Bulls deserve full respect. Although some gentle individuals can be ridden by children, other bulls are quite capable of killing you—bowling you over at full charge, goring you with their horns, trampling you with their feet, or simply crushing you with their considerable weight against a fence or wall. Bulls of dairy breeds are the most dangerous, especially when with a group of cows. Any bull can become aggressive if you unwittingly invade its fight-or-flight space or infringe some other code that a good stockperson would have respected.

In theory, if you are caught out in the open with an angry bull heading rapidly in your direction, you should run *down*hill. A bull's front legs are usually shorter than its hind legs, which means that it can go full speed *up* a slope but is less nimble on the way down.

If the sign on the gate says "Beware of the bull," believe it. Better safe than sorry.

This bull is a Hereford, usually a placid breed. Bulls of dairy breeds are far less predictable, but all bulls should be treated with respect, especially when the head goes down and the dirt starts flying!

Chapter 1

The Cattle World

Cows are bovines; they are related to a wide family of other bovines ranging alphabetically from the anoa of Sulawesi to the yak of Tibet. Wild cattle and their domesticants include:

African buffaloes (genus *Synceros*): Cape buffalo and forest buffalo.
Bison (genus *Bison*): American bison or buffalo; European bison or wisent.
Asiatic buffaloes (genus *Bubalus*): domestic water buffalo (swamp and river); lowland anoa and mountain anoa; tamarao.
True cattle (genus *Bos*): wild aurochs (extinct); domestic humpless and humped cattle; banteng and domestic Bali cattle; gaur or Indian bison and domestic gayal or mithun; kouprey or Cambodian forest ox; yak, both wild and domesticated.

One of the attempts to "recreate" the extinct wild aurochs is only a look-alike mixture of older breeds. *Wolfgang Rueckl, Shutterstock*

Wild ancestors

The now-extinct aurochs (*Bos primigenius*) is the ancestor of domesticated true cattle all over the world, except for the localized Bali cattle, the gayal or mithun of Assam and Burma, and the yak.

The wild aurochs (plural: aurochsen) inhabited a huge area, right across Asia, Europe, and North Africa, but it never reached the American continent. In Asia and Africa, the wild races became extinct perhaps 2,500 to 3,500 years ago; in Europe, the species lasted considerably longer and the last known wild cow was killed in Poland in the seventeenth century.

This splendid beast, seen in ancient cave paintings, sported enormous horns of various shapes and powerful neck muscles to support their weight. In Europe, the bulls stood as high as 6 feet (1.8 m) at the shoulder; their coats were black, with

Opposite: The American bison. *Sebastien Burel, Shutterstock*

a pale stripe along the spine, curly white hairs on the top of the head, and a white ring around the muzzle. The cows were usually reddish. Some three hundred years after the death of that last known wild cow in Poland, a few people tried to recreate the aurochs by crossing various domesticated breeds until they achieved animals that *looked* roughly like the ancestor. Of course, the resemblance was only superficial. A lot has changed in the long millennia of domestication.

all had long horns. Archaeologists have found horns more than 2 feet (61 cm) in length and 9–10 inches (23–25 cm) in circumference at the base. In some areas, the animals were gradually bred for shorter horns, but this occurred rather later in history—evidence indicates that short-horned cattle existed more than 5,000 years ago, and these would become the dominant type in most of Europe. The shorthorns also became increasingly smaller animals as domestication progressed.

Domestication

There is evidence of the existence of domesticated cattle some 8,500 years ago in southern Turkey and elsewhere. The ancient domesticants, like the aurochs itself,

Following the trail

Although local aurochsen were likely domesticated gradually by different peoples in different parts of the species' wide range, those domesticants also followed

The American Brahman originally was developed from old Asian humped breeds, especially Indian zebu.

human migrations, which took them into different regions and continents often thousands of miles from their homeland. And in their new surroundings, they began to evolve in different ways.

Local preferences did not just determine horn length and shape or the color of the coat. There was also the matter of "the hump." The aurochs had no more of a hump than the typical "crest" found between the head and shoulders of bulls in most European breeds, but in warmer regions this crest gradually developed into a hump—partly as a matter of human choice, but no doubt also because of environmental factors in new climates. Humped cattle are typically seen in Asia and Africa, and have more recently been

African affinities

In parts of Africa, cattle have played a vital role not only economically but also culturally and in ritual ceremonies, especially among the great nomadic pastoralists such as the Masai and the Fulani. Some peoples used their cattle as bride wealth. Animals were exchanged on marriage, not as a way of "buying" a wife but more as a guarantee that she would be a good one. If it all went badly wrong, the cattle that the bridegroom had given her family in trust must be returned to him. Cattle also represented status and wealth, which meant that numbers (a chief's influence could be judged by the vastness of his herds) and good looks were more important than productivity. The owner might prefer a certain coat color or pattern or dramatic horns.

Horns were often selected for their dramatic proportions, such as in the Ankole that can be seen in American zoos. In the past, horns were so admired that sometimes they were trained into amazing shapes—intertwined in a spiral, or arched with tips meeting, or persuaded to go in odd directions (one forward, one back for

The typical horns of this East African Ankole cow are massive.

example, or one heading skyward and the other earthward), or even incised in a very young animal so that it appeared to grow four (or more) rather than two horns.

Sometimes the cattle were used as draft animals, and in some cultures they were ridden. Meat was not often the reason for owning cattle. More often, it was milk that formed a major part of the diet, though in some cases fresh blood was taken from the living animal on a regular basis, rather like tapping a maple for syrup.

imported by North and South American cattle breeders as well.

Archaeological evidence suggests that humped cattle originated east of Mesopotamia and eventually spread to India and southeast Asia in one direction and to the eastern Mediterranean and Africa in the other. In Africa, several major types of domestic cattle migrated across the continent and sometimes mingled. They included the ancient giant-horned and lyre-horned humpless animals of North Africa and Egypt, humped cattle from India, and some humpless short-horns that ultimately made their way to southern and West Africa.

Cultured cattle

In many parts of the world, both ancient and modern, cattle have been respected to the point of veneration. In others, they have been respected but at the same time tortured and sacrificed.

On the Mediterranean island of Crete in ancient times, a favorite sport was bull-jumping. To prove their courage, men ran head-on toward a charging bull and seized its long horns to somersault on to its back and then land on the ground beyond. No doubt this activity was a forerunner of Spanish bullfighting, in which the bull was teased to fury and then tortured with darts and finally stabbed to death in the ring.

Hathor, the ancient Egyptian goddess of love, music, and dancing, was usually represented as a cow. *Bill McKelvie, Shutterstock*

An ancient religion in which bull sacrifice was integral was that of the pre-Roman Celtic Druids. They would sacrifice white bulls, and white cattle retained an almost mystical importance in many Celtic areas, especially Wales and Ireland. White cattle with colored ears (preferably red) were the subject of pre-Christian Irish epics dated back to the fifth century BC.

In contrast to bulls, cows have often been recognized for their generosity and gift of life and nurture. Ancient Egyptians worshiped several cow goddesses.

Cows have always been important on the Indian subcontinent and are mentioned frequently in the region's literature. The generous, fecund, and maternal cow became a mother goddess at least five thousand years ago, and she also represented bounteousness such as rainfall, watercourses, and the dawn. By the sixth and fifth centuries BC, the concept of avoiding injury to living creatures began to emerge at the same time as Buddhism and Jainism, and the Brahman students of the Veda gradually assimilated the idea of the sacred cow. But it would be some ten centuries before such respect for the cow spread more widely through the Hindu community. Visitors to India today can still see much evidence of that respect, with cows amiably chewing their cud in the midst of heavy traffic, safe in the knowledge that drivers will neither harm nor harass them. As Mahatma Gandhi put it, "We have a use for the cow. That is why it has become religiously incumbent on us to protect it."

In parts of Europe, the attitude was somewhat different. In some Alpine re-

A cow goddess is displayed in an Indian temple. The statue represents a typical Indian gray-white zebu, though the long ears have been knocked off. Cows remain highly respected in India today. *Taolmor, Shutterstock*

gions, for example, cows were encouraged to fight each other at local festivals, and of course in Spain, bulls were encouraged to "fight" matadors and pay the price in blood. In the United States, the rodeos pay little heed to the dignity of the bovines that are ridden and roped, and the ranchers pay little heed to the individual sensibilities of their stock. In both Europe and the United States, cows have been exploited on a huge scale in the milking parlors to churn out increasingly voluminous amounts of milk from increasingly enormous udders that are a gross exaggeration of what nature intended. Somewhere along the line, humans in some parts of the world lost their respect for cows as individuals.

Old World and New

Today in the Old World, the humpless breeds dominate in temperate climates and the humped breeds in the warmer climates, with a mixture of intermediate humped/humpless crosses in between. Africa makes a particularly interesting canvas for those studying how the different types have spread with human migrations and evolved in their own niches.

The New World had no indigenous aurochs and hence no indigenous domestic cattle. It was wide open to introductions by assorted waves of ocean-borne human settlers, especially those from different parts of Europe. French and (particularly) British cattle quickly populated much of the eastern United States, arriving with the early settlers and accompanying them on later migrations westward; likewise, Spanish and Portuguese cattle found their way into the southern states and into Central and South America. In the past century or so, the cattle of Asia and Africa have become increasingly influential as well; more recently, there has been an influx of lesser-known European breeds, along with some newcomers from Australia. All of these resources have helped in the development of new breeds that can genuinely be described as American.

Ferals and island cattle

Whenever the Europeans wandered the oceans in search of new lands and new resources, they tended to bring a few livestock on board to supply fresh food during the voyage and to stock those new lands once they found them. Very often, they also dropped off a few animals on various islands along the way, leaving them to forage as best they could, so that future voyagers would find a living larder when they anchored in the island bays. Sometimes, islands even became a haven for shipwrecked animals that managed to swim their way safely ashore.

An island is the ideal environment for the creation of a "breed" by the old-fashioned method of inbreeding but without a human hand to aid in selection for what to a human eye is the best. Necessarily, the breeding pool is limited, and gradually a type tends to evolve that is able to survive and thrive in the environment of that island.

In the Seychelles, the tiny island of Felicité—just 1.5 square miles (4 square km)—received a mixture of creole cattle, Friesians, and Red Sindhi zebu in 1960. The animals quickly became feral, meaning they looked after themselves without human interference. This eclectic mixture, breeding at random, gradually developed into a type that was solid black (with only a few black-and-whites but no reds) and humpless (despite humped cattle in their ancestry), with many hornless animals despite all of the ancestors being horned. In southwest Hawaii, some Mexican cattle were imported in 1793 and some British breeds came in the nineteenth century. The feral descendants of this mixture became generally small and slender—which probably has more to do with their way of life (which at one stage included being hunted) than their breeding.

On the ranges

Cattle from the Iberian Peninsula that arrived in Latin America in the early days of European settlement thrived in the climate and gradually adapted to regions that were closer to the equator than their homeland. These mixtures of Spanish and Portuguese animals were known as *criollo* (Spanish), *crioulo* (Portuguese), or *creole* (French), which means, literally, "nursling" but came to mean native but not aboriginal. Applied to humans, it meant people of European blood born in the colonized lands of America, Africa, and the Indies. Criollo cattle are those of Iberian origin in what used to be the colonies, i.e. they are descended from animals originally brought in from Spain and Portugal. These cattle were not so much breeds as local types—often those found by settlers near the ports of embarkation for their adventurous journey across the Atlantic Ocean. A factor that the Spanish and Portuguese cattle had in common was long handlebar horns.

The very first criollo cattle, a group of young bulls and pregnant heifers, made the voyage with Columbus himself in 1493, on his second transatlantic venture. He loaded cattle from the Canary Islands (settled some two decades earlier by colonists from northern Spain) and eventually landed a few of the ship's livestock at Santo Domingo (now in the Dominican Republic). Gradually, the herds in what would be Hispaniola, Puerto Rico, Jamaica, and Cuba built up with each wave of conquistadors, missionaries, and settlers. In due course, these herds began to stock Spain's colonies on other islands and on the mainland continent, initially

The Florida Cracker cow descends from sixteenth-century Spanish cattle.

in Central America and the northern coastal regions of South America in the sixteenth century, and into southern states along the U.S. coast during the seventeenth and early eighteenth centuries. Some came to the United States even earlier. Cattle are known to have been landed in Florida during Ponce de Léon's unsuccessful attempt at exploration in 1521. From these early mainland bases, they could spread easily enough into other regions, either as ranching animals or, as often as not, of their own free will. It wasn't long before huge, free-ranging herds of half-wild scrub cattle were grazing all over the savannahs, llanos, and pampas plains of South America. By the early nineteenth century, the descendants of those ancestral few numbered in the millions, spreading right down to southern Argentina and up to Mexico's old northern border just south of Oregon—and beyond.

There are still herds of true criollo cattle, but most have been improved beyond recognition by crossing with temperate European breeds or imported tropical zebu.

The King Ranch

In 1825, Richard King was born of Irish stock in Orange County, New York. As a ten-year-old, he stowed away on a schooner bound for Mobile and eventually found himself building up a successful steamboat business. In 1852, Captain King took a riding trip in southern Texas to look for land north of the Rio Grande and found what he wanted by the Santa Gertrudis Creek, an area of knee-high grass and brush ranged by feral criollo Longhorn herds. When King died of stomach cancer in 1885, he bequeathed a ranch of 500,000 acres, a massive dollar debt, and the red, thick-bodied Durham Shorthorn bulls that were the ancestors of what would one day become a famous new breed of cattle: the Santa Gertrudis.

After King's death, the ranch was managed by his widow's lawyer, Robert Justus Kleberg, who married into the fam-ily. He managed to clear the massive debt and extend the holding to 650,000 acres by the time his son was born in 1896.

A hundred years after the captain had first come upon the Santa Gertrudis Creek, the famous King Ranch covered 900,000 acres in eight counties, supporting 3,000 well-bred horses and 85,000 cattle. There was also the town of Kingsville, with 17,000 inhabitants. In 1950, when Frank Goodwyn (born 1911 and a cousin of J. Frank Dobie) returned to the ranch where he had spent his youth on the ranges working the cattle, the beasts were far su-perior to those he remembered: tough as the old Longhorns but big and beefy, dark wine-red beauties that were now the breed known as Santa Gertrudis. Goodwyn's book *Life on the King Ranch* gives a de-tailed account of daily life on the ranges and in the cowboy camps.

The pride of the King Ranch: young Santa Gertrudis bulls. The large ears are typical of breeds with Brahman blood.

Cattle populations worldwide

The Ayrshire (right) is a Scottish dairy breed that has spread to many parts of the world.

There are about 1.3 billion cattle worldwide. Of these, about 100 million are in the United States which, as a country, ranks fourth in world numbers after India (400 million), Brazil (150 million) and China (150 million). It is estimated that Africa has about twice as many cattle as the United States, and Europe has about 130 million.

Chapter 2

Looking at Cows

There are more than a thousand breeds of cattle worldwide, which might make the thought of identifying any of them alarming. To whittle it down just a little, this guide is designed to help with recognizing breeds likely to be raised in various parts of the United States.

All cattle, whatever their breed and origins, have a few basic features in common. They can run at a fair speed, albeit somewhat heavily. In some breeds, the legs are long, enabling them to range over large areas; in others, the legs are short enough for the breed to be described as dwarf. (Some are true dwarfs; others have simply been bred with short legs to ensure they put more energy into making meat than into wandering all over the place.) All cattle have cloven hoofs; that is, the foot is divided into two "claws"—a feature they share with sheep, goats, pigs, and deer.

Cows have broad muzzles, well adapted to grazing, and long tongues that curl around herbage. Most of them have broad foreheads and wide-set eyes placed to the sides of the face.

There are differences in the profile of the face. Some breeds have dished or concave faces, others have a straighter profile, and a few have very short faces with very straight profiles. Zebu have rather long, narrow "coffin" heads with a convex profile.

Cows have large ears, useful in detecting trouble and expressively mobile. In most of the Asian zebu cattle, the ears are particularly large and tend to droop. Zebu also have much looser skin than non-zebu cattle, and it often hangs in big dewlap folds under the throat and down to the chest.

Zebu have marked fatty humps over the shoulders, and this feature (though smaller) often persists in American breeds that have originated by crossing with the Brahman. Most of the European-originating breeds also have small humps but only in the bull, and this "crest" is farther forward, muscular, and much less pronounced than in zebu cattle.

At the other end, cattle have long tails with a switch of hair at the end, perfectly suited to swatting flies or clouting a pesky milker.

Adult cows have very obvious and often exaggeratedly pendulous four-teated udders. Heifers also have udders, but these can be vanishingly small. Full bulls have very obvious "tackle," especially the testicles. Bullocks, by definition, lack the latter.

Opposite: Looking at cows—and cows looking at you. A Guernsey cow investigates the camera.

Body shapes

Cattle have been bred over many centuries for different roles, and their body shapes have evolved to suit those roles.

Dairy cows are wedge-shaped, whether viewed from the side or from above. They are narrow at the front end and wider toward the rear so that they have ample space for carrying and delivering calves. They are elegant and fine-boned.

The Holstein is a wedge-shaped dairy breed.

Draft cattle were usually bred to *pull* things, and they needed weight at the front end for this. So they were bred for massive shoulders and narrow rumps. Several of the big Continental breeds now used for beef were originally draft animals.

Roan Shorthorn oxen have the right shape for working animals. *Rod Dombek, Shutterstock*

Beef cattle are bred for maximum distribution of the best cuts of meat, which are mainly in the rump and therefore their muscle mass (meat) is concentrated at the back end, but with so many different cuts in demand the muscle mass is also well distributed all over the body, giving the animal a blocky rectangular outline.

The Beefmaster is squarely bred for American beef.

Horns

Ancestral wild cattle, both males and females, always had horns. In the early domesticants, as in the original wild animals, the horns were always long.

There is immense variety in the shape, length, direction of growth, and color of horns in the modern cow. In the past, the horns were a useful indicator of what breed the cow might be, but very often now you will see cattle with no horns at all, which is often necessary for easier management and safety.

To make a cow hornless, the growth of the horns can be curtailed soon after birth by various methods involving chemicals or hot irons to kill the horn buds so that they cannot develop into horns. More humanely, breeders can take advantage of a genetic "polling" factor to breed cattle that never even start to grow horn buds.

The genetics of hornlessness are quite simple in non-zebu cattle. There is a dominant version of the gene for being polled (i.e. hornless), whereas the version for having horns is recessive. This means that if you mate a hornless bull with a hornless cow, the offspring will also be hornless. If a horned animal is mated with a polled one, some of the offspring will be horned and some polled but you can gradually breed out the horned factor over several generations.

Coat colors and patterns

The most obvious badges of a breed are the color and pattern of its coat. The coat may vary from fine and short, especially in tropical breeds, to long and shaggy in rough, tough cold-weather breeds, but the basic colors of the coat are quite easy to

A good solid Beef Shorthorn bears the roan coat often seen in this old breed.

A Dutch Belted cow and her calf both have the distinctive white band of a belted breed.

"fix" in a breed. Typical colors range from black to gray and white, and a wide range of reds and yellows (which are actually diluted red). A **roan** coat is one with a mingling of individual colored hairs (black or red) and individual white hairs, giving a fuzzy look. This coat can be seen in particular in the Shorthorn and is not the same as a patterned coat, which has blocks of color and blocks of white.

In some places, breeders had a strong color preference for simple solid black, red, blonde, brown, or white; in others, they liked patterns—very often patches of white on a colored background, or specific areas of white (such as the face), or a white **belt** around the body in contrast to the basic coat color. In a **pied** coat, the basic color is red or black broken by clearly defined patches of white.

Some breeds are typified by a shaded gradation of color. The coat over the main part of the body may be white or light gray, or brown perhaps, then it shades gradually to a very dark color over the shoulders, head, rump, and legs.

Guernsey cows have pied coats, in this case golden tan broken with areas of white, as seen in the typical Guernsey cow on the left. Her black-and-white companion is a Holstein.

Color-pointed

One of the most intriguing coat patterns, sometimes given almost magical meaning, is the "color-pointed." This is very like the markings on a Siamese cat. The basic coat is white, but the extremities or "points"—typically ears, muzzle, fetlocks, switch, and hoofs—are black or red. Pale freckles of color are usually sprinkled over the face and shoulders as well. The skin under the white coat is usually pigmented. Breeds such as the ancient White Park cattle in Britain have made this pattern their own, but it also crops up at random in several African, Indian, and Scandinavian breeds.

Color-pointing is one end of a cline of coat pattern. A cline is a gradual change in a characteristic within a breed. The more widely the colored freckles spread on the coat and the larger they become, the more the coat tends toward becoming "color-sided," ending up with mostly color, so that the white is relegated to the back and belly. The extreme of this cline is a cleanly marked white stripe broadening along the back toward and over the rump and under the belly, in contrast to sides that are solidly colored (rather than the muzzy coloring of extensive freckles).

A White Galloway cow shows the color-pointed extreme seen also in White Park cattle.

Chapter 3

On Being a Cow

One of the herd

Like other herbivores, cows are prey animals in the wild. Their behavior has evolved to reduce the risk of being attacked and eaten. They are happiest in a herd (safety in numbers), and within that herd they establish a network of relationships, giving the herd social cohesion. And, yes, cows very definitely do have best friends. It is stressful for a cow to be introduced into a new herd, and she needs a while to sort out her own position in the herd. Cows have a "bunting order."

They will "bunt" or butt an animal who is lower in the order, just to keep them in their place. The bunt is rarely vicious. It is often no more than a nudge.

Cows have a great sense of order in all aspects of their lives. They are matronly creatures of habit; they like everything to be familiar and easygoing; they take things slowly and deliberately. They don't like to be rushed; it upsets them, makes them edgy and worried, and turns them ornery.

But they also have a strong sense of curiosity and, quite often, a sense of humor.

Two Guernsey cows indulge in an amicable bunt.

Opposite: A Holstein cow poses with a wreath. An old European folktale claimed that cows could talk at Christmas, but only children could understand what they were saying!

A group of heifers will be curious about absolutely everything—and sometimes their curiosity is interpreted as menace. It's not. They just need to know, and if they notice something unusual they want to investigate it.

Body talk

Cow body language is easy to read if you take the trouble to stand and watch. When a cow is surprised or a bit afraid, she tends to widen her eyes. When she's really worried, she might become skittish and snort a bit, though that could be just playful. When she's seriously annoyed, she'll probably put her head down and look menacing. If she starts pawing the ground like a bull, get out of there.

While you're leaning over the gate watching cows, you will notice that they kneel on their front legs before lying down, and they push up with their back legs first as they rise. Cows never sit on their haunches. At rest, they are usually lying on the sternum with the front legs tucked under the body. To sleep, they remain in that position but often turn their head back along the body toward the flank. Cows don't lie on their backs, and you rarely see a cow lying stretched out on her side. If you do, it's only for a short while—or because she's dead.

A cow's favorite pace is the amble, although cows are quite capable of running. When they are first turned out on grass after a winter of confinement, even the oldest of the herd will scamper and prance across the turf, kicking up her heels and cavorting about the place like a young heifer.

Cows can also scoot crazily—tails held high—if they are being pestered by gadflies.

If necessary, cows can jump, and often do if they are being chased or if there is something interesting on the other side of the barrier. They can also

A Holstein cow struggles to her feet, back end first in true bovine fashion, taking care not to trample her own enormous and unwieldy udder.

swim. They actually *like* water, and they enjoy wallowing in it.

The senses

Smell is the most important sense to a cow, which is why you often see a cow sticking her tongue up her own nostrils to keep them moist. Smell helps her to select the choicest grazing, to be aware of approaching predators, and to know the state of mind (and body) of another cow in the herd. The sense of hearing is also

What's in a moo?

Cows communicate with each other mostly just by being there and by expressing body language and grooming each other. But they also have voices, and these can carry over considerable distances—even miles.

If you are late for the morning milking, your family cow will let you know about it in no uncertain terms by calling, just the odd low moo at first, then a bit more often, and finally a very demanding raised moo to get you out of bed.

A cow separated from the rest of the herd will also moo persistently to establish contact. A cow separated from her own calf makes a most heart-rending moo, on and on and on for hours on end, with increasing desperation, until eventually she wears herself down to a mournful foghorn sound and finally gives up on it.

But the loudest of all is when a cow is bulling—wanting to be mated. There is a special tone to the bulling moo. It is similar to the bray of a donkey, and it persists almost without a grazing break for two days. Its aim is to alert any bull within shouting distance that she is ready to meet and mate. In the wild, bulls do not live with the cows—but they soon come running when a cow shouts.

A Barzona cow calls. As she is a mixture of European breeds with African sanga and Indian zebu, her bawl is probably halfway between a moo and a zebu's characteristic bellow.

The most delightful of cow sounds is the soft muttering moo that she makes to her calf, a low, rumbling, conversational, reassuring, concerned sort of moo that is private between them, more an *mmmm* than a *moo*. If you are very lucky, she will hold a somewhat similar conversation with you at milking time if she knows you very, very well.

Moistening the nostrils heightens the sense of smell. *Brad Whitsitt, Shutterstock*

important. The large ears can move independently of each other to catch the direction of a sound. A cow's eyesight is useful on a panoramic basis. She has a wide peripheral range and can glimpse a predator anywhere from dead ahead to almost dead behind without moving her head. But she won't see clearly, more of a blur, a vague sense of what an object is (she is also partially colorblind). A cow will recognize a familiar person visually by the way they move and behave rather than recognizing their face! Add the sense of smell and she'll know exactly who you are at quite a distance. She will even recognize you after a long absence, possibly years, and if she liked you in the past she will greet you quietly—she won't rush up to you joyfully like a dog, but she'll be happy for you to come to her. If she did not like you in the past, she won't have forgotten. . . .

Eating and drinking

Cows are basically grazers. They like grass and herbs. They also fancy the occasional browse, which is to say they will chomp on shrubbery and tree foliage. They graze by wrapping their long tongues around

the grass and pulling. They don't have any top front teeth to nibble with, so they tear the grass by gripping it between their lower teeth and the hard top gum. They chew it with their grinder-like back teeth. Then they swallow, but it's only been partly chewed at that point, so they bring the food, or cud, back up again for further chewing. As prey animals, they need to be able to harvest as much food as they can as quickly as they can and then store it internally until they have the leisure to digest it when it is safe to do so.

A cow has four stomachs! The first destination for the partly chewed food is the capacious rumen, able to store food in bulk, where lots of cow-friendly bacteria get to work on the little lump of food until she is ready to belch it back up for further chewing. And then the next bit. And so on. This process is when a cow ruminates, usually with her eyes looking half-dreamy, and her occasional soft belch is of breath fragrant as new-mown hay.

One of the four stomachs, the reticulum, is a dustbin. It is where indigestible things like nails and bits of wire end up.

Cows need longer pasture than sheep and horses, so that they can wrap their tongues around each mouthful.

Cows drink water copiously but always slowly, like everything else in a cow's manner. When you consider how much milk a modern dairy cow yields, you can understand why she needs to drink so much. Milk is, after all, mainly water.

Bulling

When you are cow watching, you might see a cow acting restless, pushing her head against other cows, grooming them more often than usual, and more specifically resting her chin on another cow's rump. You might even see her rearing up clumsily on her hind legs and landing her front end on top of that cow's rump. Usually the target cow moves away abruptly and the rearer lands untidily back on all fours, looking a bit of an idiot. But sometimes the target stays still and doesn't seem to mind. This performance is an indication that one or other of the cows is "in season," ready for the bull. The target cow that moves away indignantly is not in season, but the target that stands still probably is. The rearing cow might be in season herself, or might know that the target is. One of the reasons for this mounting business is that, in the wild, the distant bull could *see* something was up, as well as hearing all that bawling.

Pregnant cows

Many cows these days never meet a bull in all their lives. They suffer the indignity of artificial insemination, with someone in a white coat lifting the cow's tail and shoving a great big syringe into its back end.

The main sign that a cow is successfully pregnant is that she doesn't come bulling again three weeks later. In due course, she will swell noticeably, and just before the birth her udder will begin to swell as well. The average length of a cow's pregnancy is much the same as a human's.

Cow basics

❖ Normal temperature: 101.3–103.1° Fahrenheit (38–39°C)

❖ Normal respiration rate: 12–15 breaths per minute

❖ Normal heartbeat: 45–60 per minute

❖ Normal adult teeth: 8 incisors (none on upper jaw), 12 premolars, 12 molars

❖ Number of stomachs: 4 (rumen, reticulum, omasum, abomasum)

❖ Likely age of heifer at first bulling: 6–14 months, depending on breed

❖ Duration of oestrus: 6–26 hours

❖ Time of ovulation: 10–15 hours after end of oestrus

❖ Interval between heat periods: 18–24 days (average of 21)

❖ Average length of gestation: 280 days

Chapter 4

On Being a Calf

Shortly before the calf is due, the cow's instinct is to withdraw from the herd and find a secret place to give birth.

When a calf is born, it is almost immediately up and running. It needs to be ready to escape from predators even in its first day of life. And with four legs to sort out, the first few hours can be quite a challenge. Once it has gained a modicum of control over those gangling legs, the calf's urge is to suckle—a very hit-and-miss affair at first. It will lurch around latching on to anything, until at last it finds one of the four teats on offer and sucks out its first postnatal meal.

A very young Brangus calf has typical Brahman ears almost too big for its head.

Opposite: A Randall Blue Lineback calf.

That first meal is crucial to the calf. The milk for the first few days is a rich yellow colostrum, loaded with antibodies that provide vital protection against disease.

In the wild, the newborn calf will hide in undergrowth and the mother will return at intervals to suckle it every few hours. The lucky calf is the one that stays with its mother for several months, learning all about life from her and other members of the herd. A new calf is always a source of great interest to the herd, and they will react as one body to protect it if threatened.

The unlucky calf is born in a dairy herd. Here, the cow's milk has a monetary value, and as soon as the mother is no longer delivering colostrum, the calf will be separated from the cow so that she

A Texas Longhorn mothers her calf.

can rejoin her sisters in the milking parlor and have all her milk sent to the cooling tank. The separation is always highly traumatic for both calf and cow. From then on, the calf has to rely on humans for its sustenance, either in the form of bottle feeding or, worse, having to lap milk from a bucket. Lapping is not what young calves are designed for.

Sucking is, and they will suck anything in compensation—including each other and your fingers.

One of the unrecognized problems of dairy calves is that they have no experienced animals to teach them—no cows to teach them about dangers, about good and bad things to eat, about how to behave in a herd or in human company.

A protective Guernsey mother stays close to her very young calf.

Chapter 5

The Generous Cow

In a survey published in 2007, it was revealed that thousands of British schoolchildren thought that cows laid eggs—and that bacon came from sheep. Only 3 percent of children living in urban areas knew that burgers came from cows, compared with a shameful 8 percent even in rural areas. Ah well, at least they *all* knew that milk came from cows; that is, those who didn't think it was made in bottles and cartons.

The docile ox

Cattle are still used in many parts of the world to pull carts, draw plows, raise water from wells, carry packs, and even,

The old red breeds of western and southern England, such as the Devon and the Sussex, were traditionally used as draft oxen in North America as well as in their homeland.
Astrid Maria Crumbly, Shutterstock

Opposite: An Ayrshire cow.

in some cases, be ridden like horses. Typically a draft animal is an ox—a castrated bull. Oxen are placid, easy to train, stolidly reliable, strong, and have great staying power.

Beef

One advantage of oxen for farm work was that, once they grew too old to be useful, they could be eaten. Most beef today comes from young animals, whose meat is more tender.

The most "natural" way of raising a beef animal is from herds in which cows are mated to a beef-breed bull and rear their own calves through to weaning. In more intensive systems, calves are removed from their mothers and raised on milk replacers fed by bucket or from teated bottles and weaned very early on to concentrates and hay.

Weaned calves may be fed on grass and concentrates, either in the field or in yards and barns, and fattened to an appropriate weight and body conformation for slaughter. In more intensive systems, they may spend their entire lives loose-housed in barns or in huge dirt lots, with any grazing material cut and brought to them.

Tallow

Fat on an animal used to be highly valued. It was a rich source of dietary energy,

A Beefmaster bull stands his ground. His roan coat and short horns suggest the Shorthorn parentage in this breed.

especially for laboring people living in colder climates. Fat, or tallow, was also a major fuel for lighting. It was the basic material from which candles were made. So in the eighteenth century, cattle were deliberately bred for a covering of blubber several inches thick. Today the situation is reversed and they are bred for lean meat.

Hides and horns

Tallow candles were often placed in lanterns with panes made from the horns of the animals that had supplied the tallow. Horn could be pared and beaten down to thin translucent panels that let the light gleam through while protecting the flame from passing breezes.

Cowhide is a basis for leather and is a major product for the cattle industry. For every dead cow in the slaughterhouse, there is a use for all the parts that are not turned into meat, and that includes the skin.

Milk and dairy products

The greatest generosity of the cow is in sharing her milk with humans. In order to give milk, she must first have given birth. The milk can then be used raw, straight from the cow, or it can be pasteurized to kill undesirable bacteria. It can be flavored; it can be condensed and sweetened; it can be shaken; it can be dried and turned into powder. It can be allowed to stand so that the cream rises to the top and is skimmed off. Milk can also be converted into a wide range of useful foods. It can be churned into butter; it can be coagulated to make every sort of cheese—an ideal way of preserving milk for many months. Natural bacteria can convert it into yogurts and various local fermented milks. Rennet, taken from the stomach of a slaughtered calf, can be used to turn milk into cheese curds.

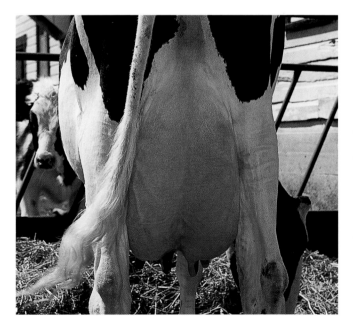

The Holstein is specifically bred to produce very large quantities of milk, hence the need for a large udder. Here, the udder is not yet full. It will be even larger, firmer, and plumper when she is ready to be milked.

Glossary

bobby. A calf up to a week old.

bovine. A ruminant animal of the genus *Bos* including, among others, cows and bulls, bison, buffalo, and yak.

brindle. A coat color streaked with another color.

bull. An uncastrated adult male bovine.

bulling. Exhibiting behavior indicating a cow is ready for mating: *a bulling cow*.

bullock. A castrated male bovine.

calf. A young bovine up to about ten months of age.

cattle. Any domestic bovine, including cows, bulls, steers, and oxen, raised for milk, meat, and draft work.

cervico-thoracic. Placed toward the neck, farther forward than a thoracic hump: *a cervico-thoracic hump*.

color-pointed. A coat pattern in which the basic color is white, with limited areas of color on the "points," or extremities (usually ears, muzzle; sometimes fetlocks and switch, occasionally scattered freckles on shoulders).

An Africander bull at home in South Africa has the typical fairly small cervico-thoracic hump of sanga cattle. *Afrikaner Cattle Breeders' Society of South Africa*

Opposite: These Hereford cows have the horns that are characteristic of the original breed.

color-sided. A coat pattern in which the sides of the body are colored (solid or mottled) and the underside, tail, and back are white; the head and legs may be white, partly colored, or colored.

cow. An adult female bovine. Also sometimes used generically to refer to a domesticated bovine of either sex.

criollo. Cattle of Spanish or Portuguese origin born in the Americas (called *crioulo* in Portuguese, *creole* in French).

crossbreeding. Mating animals of two different breeds.

dewlap. A flap of pendulous skin hanging from the throat, neck, or chest.

A Brahman bull leads the herd. The dewlap is the loose folds of skin hanging below his throat and down his chest.

dorsal stripe or **eelstripe**. A stripe of contrasting coat color (such as white, fawn, or black) along the central length of an animal's back.

finching, finchback. Broad white coat area along the back and over the tail.

genotype. The genetic makeup of an animal's cells, i.e. the particular set of genes present in its cell nuclei that determine specific traits.

grading. Crossbreeding mongrel or other-breed cows with purebred bulls and subsequent mating of their female offspring to purebred bulls to increase the proportion of pedigree blood in each generation until the level is such that the animals can be registered with the breed society.

heifer. A young cow up to and including her first calving: *a first-calf heifer*.

hybrid vigor. Increased vigor (growth, fertility, production, etc.) in the offspring of a cross between two genetically different lines (e.g. different breeds).

lineback. A coat pattern with a white stripe along the back, over the tail, and along the underside (*see also* finching).

lyre horns. Horns that are curved upward in the shape of a lyre.

ox (*plural* **oxen**). A bullock used as a draft animal (e.g. plowing, pulling wagons).

phenotype. The visible characteristics of an animal, as determined by both genotype and environment.

pied. A coat having contrasting patches of color, typically black-and-white but also white with red, brown, or yellow.

poll. A hard lateral ridge on top of the head, from which horns grow in a horned breed.

polled. Naturally (i.e. genetically) hornless.

roan. A coat color resulting from the mingling of individual hairs of two or more different colors (typically red or black hairs mixed with white hairs), with the overall effect being diffused or speckled color.

sanga. A group of cattle, originally from Africa and influenced by zebu, having a small or vestigial cervico-thoracic hump.

scrub cattle. Native feral cattle well adapted to their environment but typically smaller and less productive than farm cattle; also a term implying inferiority.

steer. A young bullock being raised for beef.

suckler cow. A cow raising her own calf.

switch. A tassel of long, coarse hairs on the tip of a bovine's tail.

taurine. Humpless cattle (*Bos taurus*), which originated in Europe and West Africa, in contrast with humped cattle breeds, which originated in Asia and parts of Africa.

thoracic. Placed above the chest and shoulders: *a thoracic hump*.

withers. The high part of the back, between the top of the shoulder blades, often used for measurement of an animal's height.

zebu. A group of cattle (*Bos indicus*), originally from Asia and later widespread in Africa and on the American continent, having a prominent thoracic hump.

Working lyre-horned zebu in India have the characteristic thoracic hump seen in zebu cattle. *Vera Bogaerts, Shutterstock*

Introduction to the Breed Profiles

Groups and categories

There are endless ways of grouping the breeds. The most basic is by type: **dairy**, **beef**, or **draft** (see "Body shapes" in chapter 2). **Dual-purpose** breeds are bred for both milk and meat; **triple-purpose** breeds are bred for milk, meat, and work.

Another grouping is by geographical origin, and within this is the more obvious distinction between the **humpless**, or **taurine**, cattle of Europe and West Africa on the one hand and the humped cattle of Asia and parts of Africa on the other. The humped cattle can be subdivided according to where the hump lies. In **zebu** cattle, the hump is thoracic (placed above the chest and shoulders)

The Jersey, an instantly recognizable dairy breed, originated from a tiny island in the English Channel but has spread to every continent in huge numbers, adapting even to tropical conditions. A Jersey herd is pictured here in Maine.

Opposite: The beautifully horned Milking Devon is listed by the American Livestock Breeds Conservancy as "Critical."

Defining a breed

In principle, a "breed" is a type that reproduces itself consistently over several generations. The consistent traits should include its phenotype, or outward appearance (such as coat and skin color and markings, body conformation, horn length and shape), and its genotype, or hidden characteristics (such as the ability to produce lots of milk or lots of beef). Thus a true breed *looks* like both its parents and also shares their qualities.

It is easy to mate a bull of one breed with a cow of another breed and produce offspring that look like a mixture of the two or nothing like either of them, but this mating does not make a new breed. A first-generation crossbred is just a mongrel. The offspring cannot claim to be a new breed until their own offspring look and behave like they do, i.e. the changes are fixed into subsequent generations. The fixing process takes many generations of careful breeding.

Nor can it be claimed that all animals with a red coat or a belted pattern or very short legs or very long horns are the same breed. They just happen to have the same coat pattern or leg conformation or horn length.

Many of the individual breed profiles include descriptions of varieties within the breed and also of ancestral breeds, or of new breeds, hybrids, or crosses that have been genetically influenced by the profiled breed. These names appear in bold for easy reference.

and prominent, and in **sanga** cattle, it is cervico-thoracic (toward the neck) and small. In the Breed Profiles, **composite** means that a breed has been developed from crosses between the basic groups (zebu, sanga, taurine) and sometimes with another species, such as bison.

Crossbreeding: Why mix them up?

The main aim in mating animals of two different breeds is to bring about hybrid vigor, and this cross is often done when all the calves are destined for meat but the mothers need to be of a "milky" enough type to rear their young. Another instance is when cows in a pedigree dairy herd are mated with a bull of a beef breed to give calves that can be sold as beef animals in due course. For example, beef buyers reject purebred male Jersey calves (a famed dairy breed). But if a Jersey cow is mated with, say, an Angus bull, her male calf will be acceptably meaty. However, the dairy farmer also wants to build up his home-bred stock of purebred Jersey heifers to come into the dairy herd in due course, and therefore he would mate some of his cows to a Jersey bull.

Creating new breeds

The traditional breeds of Europe, Asia, and Africa developed in particular home regions and were perfectly suited to environmental and social conditions in that region. In the New World, the imported traditional breeds had to adapt to strange local conditions—different climates, different diseases, different pests, different vegetation, and so on. It was often better to manufacture a brand-new breed deliberately created for those conditions, by experimentally crossing two, three, or more breeds in a long-term breeding program. There are numerous examples in the United States of such new breeds—particularly where the American Brahman (a zebu) has been crossed with European breeds.

And every now and then someone could not resist adding a different *species* to the mix as well, especially the American bison.

Some of these "new breeds" are at this stage only hybrids. The mixture of breeds has not yet become fixed to ensure that each generation is similar to the parents. Even in some of the fixed breeds, the formative mixture was so diverse that there is little uniformity in the coat color and pattern, or in other identification features such as horns.

The Santa Gertrudis evolved in Texas from a combination of Brahman (zebu) with Shorthorn (taurine). The long ears on this bull are a mark of the zebu.

Rarity

All over the world, there are breeds that are rare in their native lands. Often this scarcity occurs because the purpose for which they were originally bred has been superseded—they have gone out of fashion and other breeds can do it better. In some countries, organizations such as the American Livestock Breeds Conservancy (ALBC) seek to protect their rare breeds. The ALBC categories are:

Critical: Fewer than 200 registrations per year in the United States, and estimated global population less than 2,000.

Threatened: Fewer than 1,000 registrations per year in the United States, and estimated global population less than 5,000.

Watch: Fewer than 2,500 registrations per year in United States, and estimated global population less than 10,000.

Recovering: Previously listed in any of the above categories and have now exceeded "Watch" category numbers but still need to be monitored.

Feral: Known to have been running wild for at least one hundred years with no known introduction of outside blood.

In 2006, the ALBC listed eight "Critical" breeds of cattle, five of which (Canadienne, Florida Cracker, Milking Devon, Pineywoods, and Randall Lineback) were unique to North America. They also listed one "Threatened" breed (Red Poll), five "Watch" breeds, and four "Recovering" breeds.

Using the breed profiles

The main part of this book is devoted to profiles of all the breeds you are likely to see raised in the United States. For each breed, or group of breeds, there is a short history and a photograph. There is also a description of the breed's features and other details to help you to identify them in the field. The main features to look out for are coat color and patterns, the shape and length of horns (if any), the type of hump (if any), the general shape (body conformation) of the animal, and the purposes for which it is being used. The following features are listed under the general description where they might be helpful:

Type (zebu, sanga, taurine, or composite)
Uses (e.g. for production of milk or meat)
Coat (color, patterns, texture if important, skin pigmentation if unusual)
Horns (length and shape if significant, or natural lack of horns in polled breeds)
Body (including size if particularly large or small, special body conformation such as double-muscling, hump if a feature of the breed)

Alternative breed names are given where useful. Varieties of the main breed are also included where relevant.

It is important to bear in mind that the animals you see may have marked differences to the formal characteristics of the breed. This is particularly true with horns. In the field, at shows, and in breed society photographs, an animal that has no horns is not necessarily of a naturally polled breed or variety. Many cattle raisers deliberately prevent the incipient growth of horns while the animal is still a calf. Others introduce the genetic polling factor for hornlessness into their own herds (either by exploiting a natural mutation or by using sires of a naturally polled breed), and this practice is now widespread in several major breeds that are traditionally horned.

Another identification trap is the immensely varied characteristics in new breeds, types, and hybrids created by crossing several different breeds and even different species. They have not yet settled into the uniformity that is usually the badge of a breed, and indeed some breeders concentrate more on performance criteria, seeing appearance as unimportant.

Opposite: The rare Randall Blue Lineback is on the ALBC "Critical" list. The blue roan (or brockle) coat color and white back are characteristic of the breed, and the combination is often seen in Nordic cattle.

Breed Profiles

Africander

This South African breed originated from Hottentot cattle in the eighteenth and nineteenth centuries and has its own herdbook and breed society in its homeland, where its name is Afrikaner. It is a sanga type, which is to say that it has a small hump. In South Africa, it is usually red, but there is also a yellow strain, and it normally has long lateral horns, though a polled variety has been developed as well.

The Africander was initially exported to the United States to the famous King Ranch. In the 1950s, imported Africander cattle (30 percent) were crossed with Angus (70 percent) at Jeanerette, Louisiana, to create, over the next ten years, the **Africangus** beef breed. The Africander also played a major role in the formation of the **Barzona** in Arizona. In its homeland, the Africander contributed to the red Bonsmara of the Transvaal (along with Shorthorn and Hereford) and the shiny black Drakenberger of Natal, also known as the Black Afrikaner.

A herd of Africander cattle in their native setting in South Africa show the original breed's characteristic red coat and outspread horns. *Afrikaner Cattle Breeders' Society of South Africa*

Type: sanga
Use: beef
Coat: uniform red; short, smooth, and glistening
Horns: oval in cross-section, medium to long, straight drooping in male, horizontal in female
Body: prominent muscular cervico-thoracic hump in males; large dewlap

African Cattle

Several sanga breeds have been imported from Africa and become established in the United States, often in crossbreeding programs in which their tolerance of hot conditions and ability to make the most of sparse grazing have been incorporated into new American breeds. They include the Africander (see also Barzona), the ornamental Ankole of East Africa (see Ankole-Watusi), and the Tuli. There are other African sangas that could be useful in the United States, such as the Bonsmara (based on the Africander), the Mashona, and the N'Dama. The cattle of Kenya, improved by British colonists in the past, could also find a place in the United States, especially the big Boran zebu (one of Africa's top beef breeds), and perhaps the handsome Red Bororo zebu of West Africa.

A group of Watusi cattle in their African homeland (Rwanda, Burundi, and neighboring areas) display a good range of coat colors and patterns as well as dramatic horns. *Mike Brake, Shutterstock*

Angus

The type originated in northeast Scotland from a mixture of the old Angus Doddie and the Buchan Humlie in the late eighteenth century; it was recognized as a breed there in 1835 and was formally named the Aberdeen-Angus in 1909; this is still

Type: taurine
Uses: beef (prime marbled), early maturing; useful sire on first-calf heifers of other breeds (easy calving); passes polling gene to cross-bred offspring
Coat: solid black; skin heavily pigmented
Horns: polled
Body: blocky, fine-boned; originally small and short-legged; now longer, taller and leaner in United States

the breed's name in the United Kingdom. At first, its British herdbook (1862) also included another polled Scottish breed, the Galloway, but from 1879 the Aberdeen-Angus had its own breed society and it became perhaps the most famous prime beef breed in the world. It was exported from its native land to more than sixty countries and found great favor in both North and South America as well as many other countries worldwide. It was first imported into the United States in 1873 and has had its own U.S. breed society since 1883.

The main type is black and polled but there is a red variety, **Red Angus**, which has had a U.S. breed society since 1954 and is also sometimes called Red Aberdeen-Angus or, in South America, Aberdeen-Angus Colorado. In Wyoming, the red **Regus** herd was developed at Beckton Stock Farm, Sheridan, by grading Hereford to Angus. The black or red polled **Amerifax** was created by crossing the American Angus (5/8) with American Beef Friesian (3/8), and its breed society was first established in 1977.

Several other new breeds in the United States and elsewhere have been created with at least some Angus blood in their veins, including Africangus (see Africander), Barzona, Brangus, the Canadian composites Beef Synthetic and Pee Wee, Chiangus (see Chianina), Hash Cross (see Regus), Holgus (see Holstein), Ibagé (Brazil), Jamaica Black, Japanese Poll, Murray Grey, and Wokalup (see Charolais).

There is a red variety within the Angus, as is often the case with black breeds.

Left: An Angus cow of the original breed color, black.

Ankole-Watusi

This dramatic breed is famous for its enormous horns. It is African in origin. The Ankole cattle of East Africa have always been favored for their gigantic horns, sweeping outward and gently upward in a smooth curve like the crescent of a new moon resting on the animal's head. The Ankole is a sanga, which means that it has a small hump—in the Ankole's case, very small, almost non-existent in the cows. In its homeland around the big central lakes, it was always bred for horns and milk (an important part of the local diet) but was never eaten as meat. The colors varied according to tribal preference and included red (most common), fawn, and brown solid coats but also pied animals.

The Watusi is an Ankole type found in the Burundi, Kivu, and Rwanda area and has the most dramatic horns of all the Ankole cattle. Its tribal owners, reputed to be the tallest people in the world, were famous "cattle warriors." The horns of Watusi cattle can be as long as 60 inches (150 cm), their widespread tips up to 70 inches (180 cm) apart—and the very special Inyambo sacred cattle could have a horn span of 95 inches (240 cm) tip to tip. Watusi cattle are usually solid dark red, sometimes with spots or splashes of white, but can also have coats from black to brown, yellow, or white.

A few Watusi cattle were imported for exhibition in German and other European zoos from the 1920s onward, and after World War II, a few came to Canada and the United States. In 1960, two Swedish-born Watusi bulls came to the United States, followed by three cows from an English zoo three years later, and since then the Ankole-Watusi has grown in numbers in the United States, with a thriving breed association (1983) that took it out of the zoos and parks and into the rodeos and the beef ranches. There has been some crossbreeding of Ankole-Watusi with Texas Longhorn. The ALBC lists the breed as "Recovering."

A breakaway "World Watusi" Association was formed in addition to the original Ankole-Watusi International Registry.

Type: sanga
Uses: ornamental; dairy (very high butterfat), beef, rodeo
Coat: smooth, often solid deep red; also spotted with white; also various other colors
Horns: dramatic and huge, usually sweeping out and up, but also outward or in a circle
Body: graceful build, small hump, very long tail

The Ankole has been selectively bred in Africa for centuries for huge horns; the Watusi variety's horns were always the most dramatic.

Aubrac

This is originally a French breed from the Aveyron-Lozère region, where it was established before the end of the nineteenth century as a triple-purpose breed. It had originated two centuries earlier at a Benedictine abbey and was later "improved" with infusions of Shorthorn, Highland, Devon, and Swiss Brown. As a result of a French conservation program, by 1980 there were 60,000 breeding cows in France but the breed had suffered severely from brucellosis, a disease that causes spontaneous abortions in cows, which infected 20 percent of the animals (four times as high as any other French breed). It is also known as the Laguiole.

Type: taurine
Uses: beef; also draft and dairy (useful suckler cow)
Coat: fawn to brown
Horns: middle length
Body: sturdy

The bulk above the shoulders of this good beefy Aubrac bull is its crest; it is not a hump as seen in zebu cattle. *Eric Grant, Wahoo! Productions, Inc.*

Ayrshire

This old dairy breed from southwest Scotland has spread worldwide and become a particular favorite in the Nordic countries but also in the hotter climates of parts of Africa and South America as well as Australasia. It originated in the late eighteenth century from local cattle crossed with the Teeswater (Shorthorn) and other breeds, with a little Highland blood added in the nineteenth century and no doubt a dash of Alderney and Jersey as well. Bred as an efficient milk producer, the Ayrshire also became a famous show ring cow in Britain, known for its well-shaped udder, daintily graceful lyre-shaped horns, and attractive coat color. First imported into the United States in the 1820s, probably into Connecticut, it soon became popular in New England and a breed society was formed in 1863. In the 1920s, Ayrshire dairy herds were common near cities. A successful publicity stunt in 1929 featured two of the cows being walked all the way from Brandon, Vermont, to St Louis, Missouri, to prove the breed's hardiness—and then calving normally and producing outstanding milk yields. It is a long-lived breed and has contributed its desirable qualities to several breeds, especially in Scandinavia.

There are large numbers of Ayrshires worldwide, but in the United States it is on the ALBC "Watch" list.

Type: taurine
Use: dairy
Coat: defined patches and spots of reddish mahogany (pale to dark) on white
Horns: lyre-shaped, middle length
Body: medium size; dairy wedge-shaped, fine neck and shoulders, alert carriage

These Ayrshire cows look right at home in Vermont. The herd shows a good range of the breed's coat patterns.

The original Ayrshire in Scotland had beautiful lyre-shaped horns, but in most herds today the horns are not allowed to grow.

Barzona

Created by F. N. Bard in Arizona (hence the name), the Barzona is well suited to its harsh environment. The mixing of genes took many years and considerable scientific input from geneticist E. S. Humphrey. The types included in the mix were Indian zebu (Brahman), African sanga (Africander), and British breeds (Hereford, Shorthorn, Aberdeen-Angus), combined to produce heat tolerance, resistance to diseases and insects, and good ranging legs, along with the ability to make the most of rough fodder. The breed society was formed in 1968.

Type: zebu/sanga/taurine composite
Use: beef
Coat: medium red (lighter to darker), occasional touches of white on underline; skin pigmented
Horns: horned or polled
Body: medium size; long-bodied, with longish head and deep-set eyes

The Africander sanga contributed to this carefully bred beef animal. The Barzona was developed specifically for a harsh environment in Arizona.

Beefalo

Type: bison/cattle hybrid
Use: low-fat beef

The Beefalo is a bison/cattle combination (see page 69). In this case, breeders have managed to increase the fertility rate of the hybrid to such an extent that it has become a breed (a male Beefalo mated to a female Beefalo will produce a pure Beefalo calf) by keeping the proportion of bison at a maximum of 3/8; above that, the animal is still classified as a bison hybrid, not a Beefalo. The proportion can range down to 3/16 bison. The rest of the genotype comes from various cattle breeds, including Angus, Beefmaster, Hereford, Limousin, Santa Gertrudis, and virtually any other that the rancher might choose. Development began in the 1970s, and an American Beefalo World Registry was established in 1983. Appearance and size vary depending on the cattle breed used in the mix; there is not much visible evidence of bison, except for a woollier coat in some animals.

The Beefalo betrays little of its one-third bison ancestry, apart from perhaps a touch of extra wooliness in its coat, but it is capable of foraging efficiently in conditions ranging from blizzard to drought. *Skidmore Beefalo Farms*

Beefmaster

Tom Lasater, a thoroughly practical cattleman in southern Texas, methodically began to create his Beefmaster in the 1930s, ruthlessly culling until he achieved his ideal stock animals. These creations turned out in due course to be a mixture of Hereford (1/4), Shorthorn (1/4), and Brahman (1/2). The ranch moved to Colorado in 1954, but the breeding policy continued, and a breed society was formed in 1961. The appearance is variable; what counts is performance and profitability.

Type: zebu/taurine composite
Use: beef
Coat: variable but usually dun or red-brown, sometimes small white markings or pied; also yellow, black, brindle
Horns: horned or polled
Body: small hump in male

Top: A Hefty Beefmaster bull has a dewlap inherited from the Brahman and stubby horns from the Shorthorn.

Above: A Beefmaster heifer shows the most common color in this zebu/taurine commercial breed.

Belgian Blue

The development of this extraordinary European breed began in the 1840s, when British Shorthorn bulls and Dutch Black Pied bulls were mated with local red or red-pied cows in central and southern Belgium to improve the type. A herdbook was established in 1919, after which the animal was developed as a dual-purpose breed until the 1960s, when it was instead turned into an extreme beef type with the unusual and very obvious characteristic of "double muscling" that makes the animal look like a full-time bodybuilder, especially around the thighs. This body conformation means a lot of lean beef but can make calving a big problem for the cows, often requiring caesarean section. A breed society was established in the United States in 1988. The various names by which the breed is known in different countries include Belgian White-Blue, Belgian Roan, Belgian White and Blue Pied, Blanc-Bleu, and Witblauw.

Type: taurine
Uses: mainly beef; also dual-purpose suckler cow
Coat: all white; blue; blue roan; or pied
Horns: short
Body: massive; double-muscling

The Belgian Blue's famous double-muscling sometimes creates calving problems for the cow. The breed's more common coat color is blue or blue-and-white pied, but some animals are white.

Blonde d'Aquitaine

This breed is quite a recent creation in France, recognized in only 1962 and formed by combining several old Pyrenean breeds, which means some variation still occurs within the breed. It absorbed, for example, the Garonnais and the Quercy (both beef-and-work types with turned-down horns), the Villard de Lans milk-and-beef cow, the Pyrenean Blond, and the white Mézenc. It is sometimes known as the Garonne or the Aquitaine Blond. It was introduced into the United States in 1971.

Type: taurine
Use: beef
Coat: fawn yellow to yellow-brown, sometimes with reddish tint, usually pale muzzle
Body: large
Horns: short to middle length, blond with dark tips

The Blonde d'Aquitaine is a large French breed combining several old yellow-brown or white mountain breeds with a little touch of Limousin.

Braford

The white face of the Braford, as well as its name, highlights its Hereford parentage (5/8); the remainder is Brahman. It originated when Alto Adams Junior began to cross Hereford bulls on Brahman cows at his ranch in Florida in 1947 (his huge herd numbered 5,000 cows and 300 bulls). The Braford has had a breed society in the United States since 1969, and there are also Australian and Brazilian Braford breeds. However, the zebu ancestry in the Brazilian version is not the Brahman but the Nelore, an Indian breed originating from the Ongole (which was part ancestor of the Brahman). In Argentina, the Braford is also known as the Herebu.

Type: zebu/taurine composite
Use: beef
Coat: predominantly red, usually white face and some white on body
Horns: short to middle length

The Braford's white face comes from the Hereford; the calf's large ears come from the other part of the breed's ancestry, the Brahman.

Brahman

The Brahman can claim to be the first breed deliberately developed in the United States. It was the first American beef breed, and it was a clear case of lateral thinking and originality. Previously, American cattle had evolved from old European breeds that had arrived with various waves of settlers—including not just the traditional British (and to a lesser extent French) breeds such as Angus, Devon, Hereford, and Shorthorn but also the free-ranging herds of Spanish and Portuguese criollo cattle that came up from Latin America into the southern states.

The difference with the Brahman was that it included blood from the Indian subcontinent—and from humped zebu (*Bos indicus*) cattle, rather than the typical humpless European taurine (*Bos taurus*) cattle. The Indian animals were of course well suited to hot climates, and they were first introduced into Texas during the mid-nineteenth century. Some of the earliest zebu in the United States actually came to South Carolina from Egypt in 1835. Others came into Louisiana via the British government in 1854; the United States Department of Agriculture (USDA) Jeanerette Experimental Station in Louisiana would become an early source of experimental Brahman crossing programs. And a few years later, some Brahman crosses were brought into Hays County, Texas. At this time, Indian cattle were already being crossed with Durham Shorthorns.

The small hump and dewlap on these Brahman cows are typical of the breed, as are the large drooping ears.

The full glory of the Brahman is on display in this bull, with his zebu hump, large ears, and fine dark eyes.

The imported Indian cattle were basically of four regional zebu breeds: **Kankrej**, **Gir**, **Ongole**, and **Krishna Valley** (in reality a mixture of the other three). The Kankrej is also known as Guzerat, and the Ongole is also known as Nellore or, in Brazil, as Nelore. The Ongole and the KV were of the gray-white shorthorn group of draft animals; the Gir from Gujarat was a triple-purpose mottled red-and-white breed; and the Kankrej was a gray lyre-horned animal bred for work and milk. The American Brahman was developed from a mixture of these four, partly from U.S. stock imported up to 1906 and partly from animals bred in Brazil and introduced into the United States in the 1920s and 1940s. No doubt some of the foundation stock had European blood in them as well, but the gray-white black-skinned zebu phenotype predominated.

The Brahman was largely used to improve European breeds in Texas, in particular to adapt them better to the local environment. It was also used in crossbreeding programs to create some important new breeds that have since had considerable commercial success: the **Santa Gertrudis** and the **Brangus** above all, which originated in crosses with British breeds (Shorthorn and Aberdeen-Angus), and the **Braford** (Hereford), **Brahorn** (Shorthorn), **Bravon** (Devon), **Beefmaster** (Shorthorn and Hereford), **Sabre** (Sussex), and **Victoria** (Hereford), but also many others based on crosses with Italian, French, and Alpine breeds such as Charolais (**Charbray**, **Charford**), Simmental (**Brahmental**, **Simbrah**), Limousin (**Brahmousin**), Salers (**Bralers**), Maine-Anjou (**Brah-Maine**), and Brown Swiss (**Bra-Swiss**). The possibilities are endless.

In Australia, the Brahman has been used to create breeds like the **Droughtmaster**, **Mandalong Special**, and **Wokalup**. Numerous South American breeds are also based on the Brazilian zebus.

An American Brahman Breeders Association was formed in 1924, formally adopting the name "Brahman" for the breed (many other spellings and pronunciations had been in use until then). The association had registered more than 33,000 American Brahmans by 1942; forty years later, more than ten times that number were registered. The breed has spread to more than sixty countries across the world,

Type: zebu

Use: sire on local and traditional breeds for beef calves

Coat: white to black, usually light gray shading to darker at extremities on bull, occasionally red or spotted red and white or black and white (calves sometimes born red but most soon grow gray coat); skin black (including eyelids, giving good protection against sun cancer), with natural insect-repellent oils; also a red variety

Horns: widely spaced short to medium, or polled

Body: medium size but can be fairly tall and long; deep round body; strong sturdy legs; ears large, long or broad, drooping; hump large over shoulders in bull, smaller in cow, ample loose dewlap

especially in tropical and subtropical climates. The **Red Brahman**, which was developed from red Gir and Kankrej imported from Brazil, has a red or spotted coat over black or brown skin, long pendulous ears, and Gir-type horns.

The word *brahmin* is used for freely wandering zebu cattle in India. Brahma is the supreme Hindu deity, and the cow is of course sacred in India.

Brahmans are usually gray, but red spotting is also seen.

Brangus

In the increasingly crowded arena of new part-Brahman breeds in the United States, the Brangus stands out as one of the oldest and most successful—despite the unlikeliness of pairing an originally small polled black breed from the granite Grampian region of northeast Scotland with a pale humped zebu originally from India. The Brangus successfully combines the qualities of the parent breeds, including good heat tolerance and prime beef. The breeding program began in Louisiana at the USDA's Jeanerette Experimental Station in 1932, using Brahman bulls on Angus cows, and the final mix was 3/8 Brahman to 5/8 Angus. Similar breeding was carried out privately in Texas and Oklahoma in particular. A Brangus breed society was established in 1949 in the United States and later in Argentina, New Zealand, South Africa, and Australia (where breeders had their own breeding program in the 1950s, with the same proportions). There is also a **Red Brangus**, with its own breed society formed in 1956.

Type: zebu/taurine composite
Use: beef
Coat: solid black; also a red
variety
Horns: polled

The Brangus combines the qualities of the Angus (taurine) and the Brahman (zebu).

Brown Swiss

In 1869, a few brown cattle were imported from the mountains of eastern Switzerland into Massachusetts. More came into Connecticut and other New England states in the 1880s, and a U.S. breed society for the Brown Swiss was formed in 1880. After about 155 animals had arrived, an outbreak of foot-and-mouth disease put a stop to further imports. These animals became the ancestors of all Brown Swiss cattle in the United States today.

In their Swiss homeland, the brown mountain cattle were known in German-speaking parts as *Schweizerisches Braunvieh*, meaning Swiss Brown (*Braunvieh* is German for "brown cattle"). As a triple-purpose type, they had originally produced milk and meat and had also been used as pack animals. In the American breed, however, the emphasis has been on milk production since the early years of the twentieth century and the Brown Swiss developed into a taller and finer-boned dairy type. It has become one of the larger dairy breeds, scattered widely over the country; it is also popular in Canada, and is used in Latin America for crossbreeding for both milk and meat.

In the 1960s, the Swiss Brown in Europe was heavily crossed with imported American Brown Swiss cattle and the type in Switzerland and neighbouring countries began to lose its traditional triple-purpose character. Steps are being taken today in Switzerland and Germany to save the original type.

Similarly, by the latter part of the last century, some American breeders sought to regain some of the beef qualities of the original Swiss animal by way of fresh imports from Europe, and they formed a U.S. breed society for a more dual-purpose type (milk and beef) that they termed simply the **Braunvieh**.

In Texas, Brown Swiss cows have mated with Brahman bulls to form a **Bra-Swiss**.

Type: taurine
Use: dairy
Coat: gray-brown, darker shading on extremities, paler underside, pale "mealy" muzzle ring
Horns: short
Body: taller and finer-boned that sturdy ancestral Swiss Brown

Upper left: Brown Swiss cows at Shelburne Farms, Vermont. The coat coloring is not unlike that of the Jersey. The hollows in front of the hips are typical of dairy breeds.

Left: Swiss Brown cows in their native Alps have horns that are typical of the original breed.

BueLingo

Russ Bueling in North Dakota gave his name to this new breed of belted beef cattle, which originated from fourteen of his own commercial cows born in the 1970s with plenty of Shorthorn in their genes, though the influence of these cows on the final breed appears to be limited. His aim was to stamp the new breed with a belt, and assorted belted females were acquired from other herds and mated to a Dutch Belted dairy-type bull. A Chianina bull was subsequently used to introduce better muscling for beef. The BueLingo Beef Cattle Society was formed in 1989.

It is, in fact, quite simple to fix the belting gene in cattle. It is a single dominant gene. The pattern is an eye-catching one but not common. The most typical breeds are the Dutch Belted, the Lakenvelder, and the Belted Galloway. There is also a Belted Swiss Brown and a Belted Welsh, but it is the animal under the belt that counts for production—the belting factor does not make it a better or worse dairy or beef animal.

> **Type:** taurine
> **Use:** beef
> **Coat:** belted (i.e. white band around the middle)
> **Horns:** short

The BueLingo was bred for the sake of its eye-catching broad white belt.

Buffalo and Bison

The term *buffalo* causes some confusion. The true buffalo belong to the genus *Bubalus*, which includes all the domesticated water buffalo that are of such huge economic importance in Asia and also play a role in some of the Mediterranean countries of Europe and in South America. In Trinidad, several breeds of the River type of domesticated water buffalo were imported from India during the first part of the twentieth century to work on the sugar cane plantations. Later in the century, a careful breeding program developed Trinidad's **Buffalypso** meat breed, a reddish coppery-brown or black water buffalo whose meat is almost indistinguishable from prime beef. In Brazil, which has frequently imported Asian water buffalo of both the River and Swamp types, a roan meat-and-work **Rosilho** breed has been formed (it has cream hair over gray skin), for example,

The Asiatic water buffalo, seen here in Sri Lanka, has been domesticated for several thousand years and numbers many millions worldwide. It is not the same species as the fierce African buffalo (which has never been domesticated). *Paul Cowan, Shutterstock*

along with other Brazilian breeds for milk production or for meat. There are herds of water buffalo in the United States and growing interest in water buffalo for meat and for cheese-making in temperate regions—even in England!

The water buffalo has a long cow-like body, sparse hair, a long slender neck, and a long low-held tapering head; it usually has long flat horns sweeping back from the face. As its name suggests, it loves a good wallow, and its whole attitude to life is slow, ponderous, patient, and thoughtful.

The wild "buffalo" of North America is of a different genus. It is *Bison bison*, a cousin of the European bison, which means that Buffalo Bill Cody should really have been Bison Bill. The American bison has a massive low-slung head, small horns, and hefty great woolly shoulders carrying a substantial muscular hump; its body then tapers, sloping down toward the slender rump. It is a creature of the wide-open plains.

The American bison is also in a different genus than domesticated cows in general, which means in theory that the two would never even attempt to mate in the wild, and that any forced mating would result either in no viable offspring at all or in offspring that were sterile (there is a difference in chromosome numbers). This fact has not prevented several ranchers over the decades from trying to incorporate bison blood into their cattle, to take advantage of the bison's particular qualities, especially its ability to deal with harsh conditions and make use of grazing that would not support domestic cattle.

continued on next page

An American bison in Yellowstone National Park. Its whole shape and general appearance mark it out as a different species than domesticated cattle and water buffalo. *Sascha Burkard, Shutterstock*

The results have included hybrids and breeds (there is a fine line between the two) such as Beefalo, Cattalo, and the American Breed.

The **Cattalo** experiment began back in 1894 at Bobcaygeon, Ontario, when Mossom Boyd wanted to "take the fur and hump of the bison and place them on the back of the domestic ox," by crossing bison with his Angus and Hereford cattle. The experiment transferred to Wainwright, Alberta, in 1916 and a wide range of crosses were tried, including an element of yak from Tibet. The main experiments involved bison with Hereford, Shorthorn, and Holstein-Friesian cattle, and the first-generation offspring were called hybrids, but any progeny with less than 50 percent bison were termed "cattalo," i.e. a mixture of *cattle* and buf*falo*. The breeding program continued at Manyberries, Alberta, without the yak; both hybrid and cattalo males were either sterile or had very low fertility, and the females had low fertility levels but could breed. Using domestic bulls on bison cows was more successful than the other way round, but the Canadian project was finally abandoned because of the infertility of the crossbred progeny.

Meanwhile, there were similar experiments in the United States, one of the earliest engineered by Charles Goodnight in Texas, a Longhorn man, but the early breeders came up against the same problem of sterility in the first-cross male cattalo and low fertility in the female. By the 1970s, Jim Burnett in Luther, Montana, had been breeding cattalo for more than a decade, using Herefords in the cross, and his first-generation cattalo cows were usually black or near-black, occasionally brindle, with the Hereford's traditional white face. There was no bison hump, just a "muscular thickening" over the shoulders. First-generation bulls that were 75 percent bison looked more or less like bison, but smaller, and were near-black more often than the dark brown seen in bison. But the commercial value of these experiments was never proven.

The **American Breed** and, especially, Beefalo experiments have been more successful. Created for a harsh, dry environment in New Mexico by Art Jones between about 1948 and 1974, the American Breed was at first a mixture of Hereford, Shorthorn, and Charolais but eventually composed of 1/2 American Brahman, 1/4 Charolais, 1/8 American bison, and 1/16 each of Hereford and Shorthorn. Its breed society was formed in 1971, though Jones admitted that half-bison bulls were always sterile and that infertility was prevalent in bulls that had more that 25 percent bison blood. With such a mixture, its appearance is variable.

Canadienne

This attractive but rare Canadian breed from Quebec has strong similarities with the Jersey, especially about the face, but is usually much darker in color. Its French ancestors are said to have landed in Canada from Normandy and Brittany in the sixteenth or seventeenth century, and it does indeed have strong links with the Channel Islands breeds. The Canadian cow developed thereafter in relative isolation and largely by natural selection until breeders took up the nineteenth-century fashion for crossing cows with bulls of various British breeds. The Canadienne was already a profitable and well-adapted dairy cow when a herdbook for the remaining pure animals was established in 1886, but it received a setback when Ayrshires and Holstein-Friesians became popular in the early twentieth century. Thereafter its numbers rapidly dwindled despite its good qualities and despite government initiatives to save it, and it neared extinction. Its ALBC listing is "Critical." It was given a little boost of Brown Swiss blood in the 1980s.

It is also known as the Black Canadian, Black Jersey, or Quebec Jersey.

Type: taurine
Use: dairy
Coat: black to dark brown (calves brown), usually with pale muzzle ring, occasionally a little white on stomach and chest.
Horns: short

The Canadienne's dairy type is apparent in the good, tidy udder and the hip hollows.
Canadian Cattle Breeders' Association

Canadian Hybrids

In Canada, as in the United States, various breeding programs have created new breeds or simply hybrids. The Canadian ones include the **Beef Synthetic**, developed at Alberta University from a mixture of Aberdeen-Angus (37 percent), Charolais (34 percent), Galloway (21 percent), American Brown Swiss (5 percent), and other breeds. The university also developed the **Pee Wee** beef cross from a mixture of Aberdeen-Angus, Charolais, Galloway, and Hereford, selecting for low yearling weight, and a dual-purpose **Dairy Synthetic** using Holstein (30 percent), American Brown Swiss (30 percent), Simmental (6 percent), and various beef breeds.

The **Hays Converter** was bred in Calgary and originated in 1952 from Hereford bulls mated to crossbred cows (Holstein × Hereford, and American Brown Swiss × Hereford). The resulting white-faced black or occasionally red beef animals had their own breed society from 1975 but are now rare.

The **Fort Cross** evolved on Fort William Farm at Thunder Bay in Ontario from Charolais bulls on crossbred cows born from Hereford mothers put to Lincoln Red bulls. The Lincoln Red is a large nineteenth-century beef breed from eastern England that originated from Shorthorn bulls used on local cows, with an infusion of Maine-Anjou from France at some stage. It is now a rare polled breed in its own country, though it was quite widely exported and has breed societies in Canada (where it first arrived in 1825), New Zealand, Australia, and South Africa but not in the United States.

The Charolais was also used as the sire in creating the **Burwash** for beef at the Burwash Industrial Farm in northern Ontario. Various cow breeds were used, such as Hereford and Shorthorn. The **Romark** cross, as can be guessed from its name, is based on two Italian breeds: the Romagnola bull and the Marchigiana cow.

The white face of the Hays Converter is a trademark of its Hereford ancestry. *Walt Browarny, Canadian Hays Converter Association*

Charolais

The Charolais is a big, gentle cow. This French breed has been used in the creation of several new breeds in the United States.

This handsome, muscular creamy-white breed from central France, named after the Charolles district, was originally triple-purpose, used as a draft animal as well as for meat and milk, but it is now a beef breed. It evolved in Saône and Loire in Burgundy, and a little Shorthorn blood was introduced in the latter half of the nineteenth century. A breed society was formed in France as far back as 1864. It was one of the earliest of the French beef breeds to become established in the United States, where it has had a breed society since 1951. The breed first came into the country by way of Mexico in the 1930s. There is also an American **Polled Charolais**, lighter boned than the traditional type.

Widely exported, the Charolais has managed to thrive in all sorts of climates and has also been used extensively in creating new breeds. The tan to creamy white **Charbray**, for example, was developed in Texas and Louisiana in the 1930s and 1940s by using Charolais bulls on Brahman cows; the Charolais proportion ranges from 5/8 to 7/8. A herdbook and breed society were established in 1949. The **Charford** originated at Ash Fork Ranch in northern Arizona in 1952 from a mixture of Charolais (1/2), Hereford (3/8), and Brahman (1/8). A **Chargrey** cross has been developed in Australia at Cadella Park by using Charolais bulls on Murray Grey cows; other Australian creations are the **Mandalong Special** (Charolais with numerous other Continental and British breeds and Brahman) and the **Wokalup** (Charolais, Brahman, Friesian, and Aberdeen-Angus). In France in the 1960s, the **Charollandais** was formed as a milk-and-meat cross by using Charolais bulls on Friesian cows from Holland. In Nebraska, the ever-creative G. A. Boucher at Ravenna created the white to dark cream **Char-Swiss** (3/4 Charolais, 1/4 American Brown Swiss), with its own breed society from 1961, not to be confused with the Californian **Charwiss**, which is a first-generation cross from Charolais bulls on Brown Swiss cows. The **Fort Cross** (Charolais bulls on Lincoln Red × Hereford cows) and **Burwash** (Charolais on Herefords and Shorthorns) are Canadian creations.

Boucher also put Charolais into the **Beefmaker**. It comprises half Charolais with the remainder being mostly Hereford, Angus, and Shorthorn and a smattering of Brown Swiss and Brahman. Confusingly, there is also a Beefmaker breed in Australia that has nothing to do with Charolais but is based on a combination of Hereford and Simmental; its white face is proof of the Hereford input.

The Charolais' genes are also found mingled with bison genes in the American Breed and the Beefalo.

The Charolais beef breed has been established in the United States for longer than most other French breeds.

Type: taurine
Uses: beef; originally also draft and dairy; commonly used as sire in suckler herds or beef sire in dairy herds
Coat: white or cream to light wheat, with pink muzzle
Horns: round, tapering, and white
Body: large

Chianina

An immensely tall, pale Italian breed, the Chianina was a prized work animal in Tuscany in the early nineteenth century but is now a beef breed. It has probably the longest legs of all breeds—some bulls stand as much as 6 feet (1.8 m) tall at the shoulder and can weigh 3,300 pounds (1,500 kg).

In 1971, the first batch of Chianina semen was imported into the United States (at a time when foot-and-mouth regulations prevented the import of live cattle). Like many of Italy's hardy Podolian breeds, and like some of India's zebus, its coloring is striking. Its coat is usually purest white, with touches of jet black on the muzzle, switch, and hooves, and beautiful dark eyes. America quickly became enchanted by this Italian's stylish and athletic appearance. By 1987, there were more than 12,000 pure Chianina in the country and a huge number of crosses.

The bulls were used extensively to create new breeds, including the black, polled, beefy **Chiangus**, which first developed from Chianina bulls mated with Angus cows at the Tannehill Ranch in California in the early 1970s. The handsome Chiangus soon became a popular breed at the shows. The **Chiford** came from Chianina bulls used on Hereford cows; it may be pale cream, fawn, or red, with or without the characteristic Hereford white face. The **Chimaine** is based on Maine-Anjou cows. And the Chianina was used to improve the old Marchigiana in the nineteenth century.

Type: taurine
Use: beef
Coat: pure white to steel gray, black points, black skin
Body: very tall; bulls very heavy

A handsome breed from Italy, the Chianina stands tall and proud. *American Chianina Association*

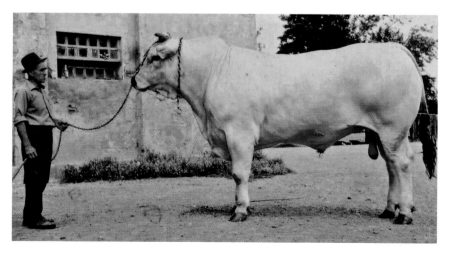

Criollo Cattle

It was in Central and South America that criollo cattle (whose introduction and spread are described in Chapter 1) became most widespread, but there are remnants of them even today in the United States, despite consistent attempts, especially in the nineteenth century, to "breed them out." Breeders tried to grade scrub cattle to north European breeds (mainly British, with some Dutch and German) that had originally been brought into the colonies by settlers and later imported in considerable numbers. The criollo were also "improved" by crossing with zebu cattle, especially the American Brahman.

Very soon, the pure criollo was a rarity in North America—but it had not quite disappeared. It could still be seen, just, in the small **Florida Cracker**, though by 1970 this type had dwindled down to a few small isolated herds, most of them with no criollo bulls to keep the gene pool alive. The biggest remnants of criollo blood in the United States are in the **Texas Longhorn**.

There are still all sorts of criollo cattle in Latin America, and some retain the typical twisting handlebars of their Spanish and Portuguese ancestors as well as their renowned docility. Even on the ranges, and

Texas Longhorn steers photographed against North Dakota's Badlands show off their characteristic handlebar horns.

despite having often been feral in earlier generations, they tend to remain calm when approached by a stranger on foot, who can come as close as about five strides before they back off—compared with a typical ranch herd of zebu running with the same criollo that will be alarmed within a flight range of 70 yards (64 m) or more. Over the centuries, the criollo have, of course, become diverse in type, affected by their environment and later by selective breeding; however, those in lowland tropical regions share the characteristics of very short, sparse coats and noticeably wrinkled skin on the neck and often on the forehead. A full range of colors and coat patterns occurs in the criollo—solid colors, speckled and spotted, color-pointed, pied, and just about anything that has ever been seen in any other breed.

There is a breed society for the **Corriente**. This term means "running" and is applied to cattle used for rodeo. The bulls originate from Spanish cattle in Mexico.

The Corriente rodeo bull comes from fighting Spanish stock.

Devon

The Devon breed originated on the damp moors of southwest England, where it tends to grow what is described as a "mossy" (dense and curly) coat against the weather. In its homeland, it is now a beef animal; it was originally also used for work. Often called the Ruby Red Devon, it came from a family of red "Wessex" middle-horned draft cattle that included the Sussex and possibly the white-backed, white-faced red Hereford. There are also links, of course, with the neighboring South Devon breed, which is larger, more yellow, and (in the past) milkier but which has some unique qualities that set it apart from the Ruby Red.

Type: taurine
Uses: beef (Beef Devon), dairy (Milking Devon)
Coat: cherry red (deep to light or chestnut), skin orange/yellow; occasionally very small white areas on underside and switch
Horns: middle length, gently curved

The Devon has spread around the world, adapting easily to hotter climates. It was an early arrival in the United States; after all, the Pilgrim Fathers set sail from the Devon port of Plymouth, and some Devon cattle landed in 1623–1624, proving their worth as draft animals that could also provide milk and meat. More came over in some numbers after the American Revolution, but its main success was later. In the nineteenth century, it was much in demand in the West as a good ranch beef breed. An American breed society was formed in 1881.

In the United States, the old breed evolved into the Beef Devon and the Milking Devon. The **Beef Devon** is now described as a "Recovering" breed by the ALBC; it lost favor in competition with other beef breeds and withdrew mainly to New England.

The old Devon moorland breed has the typical middle-length horns and deep color of the red cattle of southern and western England.

Worse, the **Milking Devon** is in the "Critical" category. The two types divided formally in the 1950s, with the Beef Devon aiming commercially at the beef market, while those who wanted to continue with the older type of triple-purpose animal, providing milk and work as well as meat, formed a separate register for their animals. They soon found themselves struggling to keep going with the old type—the type that the Pilgrim Fathers relied on for so much and that even George Washington is thought to have raised. Breeders reformed the registry for the Milking Devon in 1978; in 1985, only 15 calves were registered, though five years later the number increased to 120. The Milking Devon deserves better. She is a historic and beautiful cow, with her longish horns and deep red coat, and she makes a lovely reliable family or small-farm cow. There is also a **Polled Devon** variety tracing back to a hornless Devon bull born in 1915.

The **Makaweli**, a red Hawaiian beef breed, was created at the Robinson Ranch, Kauai, from a combination of Shorthorn and Beef Devon. The **Bravon** in Florida is a cross from Brahman bulls on Devon cows.

Check out Vermont. In 1778, the state's official seal featured a red Devon cow, and she is also featured in the state's coat of arms.

Dexter

The handy little Dexter springs from Ireland. It often comes only waist-high on its short legs; it has a broad short head and neck, and the ability to give both milk and meat economically. This small, manageable animal is a favorite family cow, but there are also commercial herds of milking Dexters and it has considerable beef potential, albeit for small joints. It has been used as a draft animal, especially in historical settings as representing what ancient Celtic cattle might have looked like.

Type: taurine
Uses: dual-purpose on small farms for beef and dairy
Coat: usually solid black; can also be red or dun
Horns: medium length, curving forward and up
Body: deep compact, low-set on short legs, shoulder height ideally 39–43 inches (99–109 cm)

The Dexter was developed from the elegant black Kerry in the eighteenth century (it is sometimes called the Dexter-Kerry) by the eponymous land agent for Lord Hawarden in County Kerry. It was exported to England in the 1880s and to the United States from 1905, where a breed society was formed in 1911. It became a rare breed for a little while, but its British numbers have recovered well through the efforts of a very active breed society and it is now considered "minor" rather than "rare"; there are also several thousand Dexters in South Africa and further populations in Canada, Australia, New Zealand, Argentina, and various European countries. In the United States it is categorized as "Recovering" by the ALBC, and there are probably more than three thousand purebred Dexters in the country.

Some lines of the breed carry a lethal or semi-lethal "bulldog" dwarfing gene. "Bulldog" calves are so badly deformed (bulging cranium, protruding lower jaw, split upper lip, swollen tongue, shortened spine, extremely short legs) that they usually die in the womb during the fifth to ninth month of the pregnancy, or die after birth from respiratory difficulties. The problem tends to occur in herds of excessively short-legged animals, which stand at about 3 feet (90 cm) and have disproportionately large heads. But good breeders, who choose the longer-legged type, have selected against this once-fashionable look. It is to be hoped that the thoroughly practical Dexter is not abused by those who seek to use it to miniaturize other breeds and turn them into pets.

Left: Most Dexters are black, but red and dun are also acceptable coat colors.

Below: Ireland's Dexter is small enough to be easily managed as a family cow, with good small beef joints for the family freezer.

Dutch Belted

The sight of a white belt around a cow's body has always been attractive for those who like their animals to look decorative in the landscape, but in only a very few breeds has a belt (the expression of a single dominant gene) been an identifying feature of the breed. One of them is the Dutch Belted, an American name for a breed that was known as the Lakenvelder in The Netherlands. The Dutch name means "sheeted field"—"sheeted" being another term for belted. The breed was exported to the United States between 1838 and 1848 (including some for the circus magnate P. T. Barnum) and in the early years of the twentieth century. To return the compliment, the American Dutch Belted went back to the home country in 1988 to help in reconstructing the Lakenvelder, which had almost been crossbred out of existence. The U.S. breed society was formed in 1868 and this dairy breed always remained pure, but a century later numbers were low—there were fewer than a thousand in the late 1980s and today they remain on the ALBC "Critical" list.

Other belted breeds include the Belted Galloway and the Belted Welsh, and white belts have also been seen within Mongolian cattle and among Indian zebu.

> **Type:** taurine
> **Use:** dairy
> **Coat:** black (occasionally red) with clearly marked white belt wrapped around body between shoulders and hips
> **Horns:** short; sometimes polled

Descended from the Lakenvelder, the Dutch Belted is on the ALBC "Critical" list. The short horns on one of these cows are typical of the old breed.

European Imports

Europe is the bedrock of American cattle. The great majority of American breeds are based on (or have substantial contributions from) imported European breeds, starting with the Spanish criollo cattle that accompanied Columbus and progressing through British breeds that came in with the Pilgrim Fathers and later settlers. Migrants from Europe often brought cattle with them from home. The European breeds continued to be topped up with imports over the centuries when politics and quarantine regulations permitted, but in many cases they gradually evolved away from the traditional type to become a recognizably American variety of the breed—often larger and taller than the ancestors.

The flow of new European blood was interrupted for many years by the fear of importing foot-and-mouth disease. After the ninth outbreak of foot-and-mouth in the United States in 1929, causing huge commercial losses, the importation of live animals from any country where the disease was known to exist was prohibited. Breeders relied on imports from Latin America and Canada.

When the use of artificial insemination became accepted, a new wave of breeds from Continental Europe began to enter the United States. Most of the importations of frozen semen came in from Canada, and the earliest of these sire breeds included the Limousin and Maine-Anjou from France and the Simmental from Switzerland. From the late 1960s,

Many European breeds have become established in North America. These Simmental cows are shown in their native Swiss mountains, where horns are still commonly retained.

some two-dozen new breeds came in via Canada after periods of quarantine. Many breeders were interested in foreign breeds, and by 1971, semen from several more Continental breeds was made available for distribution in the United States direct from Europe, where the donor bulls were held in strict quarantine, supervised by the USDA. The breeds included the Gelbvieh from Austria, the Blond d'Aquitaine from France, the "Fleckvieh" (German Simmental), the Brown Swiss, and, from Italy, the Chianina, Marchigiana, and Romagnola. This opening of the doors also led to a whole new rash of crossbreeding to make new and improved breeds.

The history of European imports is highlighted by the dates at which U.S. breed societies were created. For example, most of the English, Scottish, and Dutch breeds had their own American herdbooks and societies during the nineteenth century or early years of the twentieth, whereas most of the French, Italian, and German ones date from the late 1960s onward.

Florida Cracker and Pineywoods

A good range of coat colors and patterns can be seen on these Floridian descendants of Spanish cattle.

These small, rare creatures are the remnants of Spanish cattle from the sixteenth century, probably mixed with some random breeding with surviving British cattle of the Shorthorn, Devon, and Hereford types that ranged freely among them in these subtropical regions. Hardly surprisingly after such a long residence, these scrub cattle became ideally adapted to their environment in the southeast, with one type evolving in Florida and another in the Pineywoods region among the longleaf pine forests of the Gulf coastal plains in Georgia, Alabama, Louisiana, and Mississippi. Each type developed through natural selection of the fittest. Only those that could compete while battling high levels of humidity, high temperatures, the onslaught of assorted parasites, and minimal forage survived to reproduce.

But the biggest enemy of scrub cattle would be breeders intent on improving their native cattle in size by crossbreeding with the Brahman in the 1930s. Until then, the local cattle had remained important as they were best able to cope with the climate and surroundings, but the Brahman was equally at home there. The crossbreds were indeed bigger and more productive, and the number of purebred Spanish cattle rapidly diminished. Florida began to take steps to rescue the remnants of its scrub cattle in the 1970s, and a breed society for the **Florida Cracker** was formed in 1989. (The "Cracker" part of the name is from the sound of the cattle herders' whips; the breed is also referred to as the Florida Scrub or Florida Native.) The remainder tend to live in very small herds maintained in state parks and forests, with just a few in private hands. From thousands, they have been reduced to a few hundred, but their preservation is now in knowledgeable hands.

Likewise, a breed society for the **Pineywoods** was formed in 1999, and half a dozen family-owned strains were identified. They include Barnes, Bayliss (in Mississippi), Carter (with an unbroken family history back to the 1860s), Conway (red-and-white, Mississippi), Holt (color-sided black roan in Georgia), and Griffin (yellow). Alternative names for the Pineywoods include Southern Woods or just plain Woods.

Both the Florida Cracker and the Pineywoods are listed by the ALBC as "Critical." There is also a very rare dwarf milking variety, generally known as the **Guinea**.

Type: taurine
Use: range beef
Coat: all colors (mainly solid red, black or dark brown; also black with tan muzzle and dorsal stripe) and patterns, including color-sided and white color-pointed
Horns: less dramatic than Texas Longhorn and variable in direction and size; sometimes polled

Above: A Florida Cracker steer bears a strong pair of Spanish horns.

Left: A Pineywoods cow suckles her calf in Mississippi. *Jess Brown, Cowpen Creek Farm*

Galloway

From its southwest Scottish origins on the English borders, the Galloway has spread worldwide as a beef animal and has had its own U.S. and Canadian breed societies since 1882. It never became quite as popular as the Angus, but it is also a polled breed and is basically black (with a brownish tinge); red and dun color varieties are also recognized by the U.S. and UK Galloway breed societies. Separate breeds include the White Galloway and the well-known Belted Galloway, which have their own breed societies in the United Kingdom, the United States, Canada, and elsewhere.

Native to a cold, damp land, the Galloway can grow a shaggy rain-shedding coat with a thick, soft undercoat for insulation, but in warmer climates the coat is short. Its heavily fringed face and hairy ears are both characteristic and appealing. It is a rough, tough animal that can look after itself. The first Galloways came to Ontario in 1853 and from Canada to Michigan in 1866, with more imported direct from Scotland before a North American register was founded in 1882; U.S. breeders established a separate herdbook two decades later. The Galloway's fortunes yo-yoed over the years, and it frequently fell out of favor through no fault of its own. (Blame the breeders and their publicists!) It is now on the ALBC "Watch" list.

The **Belted Galloway**, fondly known as the Beltie and also in the past as the Sheeted Galloway or White-Middled Galloway, also appears on the "Watch" list. The Beltie is not just a color variety; it is a milkier dual-purpose strain of the Galloway and at times pure dairy herds have been formed. Its white belt is much more than a fancier's

The thick coat on the Galloway is good protection against the weather in its native Scotland. *Stephen L. Castner*

feature. It plays the thoroughly practical role of making the animals visible from afar on the hills and moors that are often their home. The first Belties came into Canada in 1939 and then direct to Pennsylvania after the war, and a breed association was formed in 1951 as imports continued. Although it is on the "Watch" list, its numbers are healthy and growing—more so than the black Galloway. It generously passes on its belt to cross-

The Belted Galloway has been bred for milk production as well as beef—it is more than just a color variety.

The most common coat color in the Galloway is black, but it may also be red or dun or, as in the background, color-pointed white.

bred calves, though not invariably; careful breeding is required even within the breed. The belt is always white and the rest of the coat is usually black but can also be dun to chocolate, or red (though the latter is not accepted by the American breed society).

The eye-catching **White Galloway**, with its colored (red, black, or dun) extremities and freckles and dark skin, fares better than the black Galloway in hotter climates. A single white heifer happened to be in a shipment of black Galloways sent from Nebraska to Montana in 1912 and her new owners developed a line of White Galloways from her that would in due course spread to Australia and New Zealand as well as other parts of North America. White Galloways were simultaneously bred in Scotland from 1919.

Type: taurine
Uses: beef (Galloway, White Galloway); dual purpose and dairy (Belted Galloway)
Coat: black, also red or dun; Belted Galloway black or dun with white belt; White Galloway white with colored points (usually black, also red or dun)
Horns: polled

The color-pointed White Galloway is better adapted to warmer climates than the original black Galloway.

Gelbvieh

The name of this German breed translates as "yellow cattle" and, accordingly, it is also known as the German Yellow. It originated from local red Bavarian beef cattle crossed with Swiss Brown and with the ancestor of the Simmental; several varieties of the type were combined under

Type: taurine
Uses: beef, dairy
Coat: yellow, ranging from creamy tan to a reddish-yellow; also a black variety
Horns: middle length, curving forward

the Gelbvieh umbrella in about 1920. It was originally a triple-purpose animal, used for work as well as meat and milk, and remains dual-purpose though increasingly bred for beef. The U.S. breed society was formed in 1971, based on Austrian imports.

The **Gelbray** was created in the United States as a beef breed from Gelbvieh bulls with Brahman cows. The Brahman proportion ranges from 1/4 to 3/8. A breed society was formed in 1981.

A young yellow Gelbvieh bull.

The name Gelbvieh translates literally as "yellow cattle," though black animals are seen in the United States.

Guernsey

The dainty Channel Islands cows from Guernsey, Jersey, and Alderney—close to the French coast but autonomous British dependencies—were already well established in American dairy herds by the mid-nineteenth century. They all had French blood but also, intriguingly, a genetic factor that connected them with African cattle (see Jersey). The word that is always used to describe the Guernsey is "golden." Her coat is a golden-brown and white, her skin is golden, her hooves are golden amber, and her butter-rich milk is a golden yellow.

The first Guernseys arrived in the United States in the 1830s and 1840s, and an American breed society was formed in 1877; by the 1920s there were some two million Guernseys in the country. Sadly, the Guernsey is fast declining in numbers, giving in to the dominance of the Holstein in the dairy world, and she has been on the ALBC "Watch" list since the 1980s.

Like the majority of European breeds, the Guernsey is naturally horned, though most dairy farmers prevent their calves from growing horns by destroying the horn buds. *American Guernsey Association*

Type: taurine

Use: dairy

Coat: light yellow to brown or red, usually broken with white

Horns: short; also a polled strain

Body: dairy type, medium size

Below: The "golden" Guernsey is another dairy breed from a small island in the English Channel, but not as famous as the Jersey.

Hawaiian Wild

In 1793, the British navigator George Vancouver landed on Hawaii's Big Island with a few cows he had bought in California. A year later he brought a couple more cows and three young bull calves, all described as black New Albion. At the same time, some longhorn criollo cattle were brought to Oahu from Mexico. In due course, these various groups mingled, lived wild, and quickly grew in number—so much so that these Hawaiian "wild" cattle caused considerable damage in the forests and became a target for hunters. But these well-adapted scrub cattle were also crossbred with British beef cattle such as Angus, Hereford, and Shorthorn in the nineteenth century and ranched on a huge scale, serving an export market in beef and hides, until eventually pure beef and dairy herds replaced them. By the 1970s, the Hawaiian Wild was reduced to a mere handful of individuals in remote mountain areas, and steps were taken to preserve what remained.

Feral cattle had been exterminated deliberately on Maui and Oahu because they were a source of tuberculosis; and in theory they were also hunted to extinction on Molokai in the 1950s, though herds were reported there in the 1980s. Remaining ferals on Kaui appear to be mainly of Hereford and Shorthorn ancestry. On the Big Island, most of the ferals in the 1960s (and there were many of them) also appeared to be descended from Hereford range cattle, but on the mountains on southern Mauna Loa they were different, and a small herd of a dozen cows and a single bull were maintained in isolation from ranch herds, unmanaged except for replacing the original bull with a Texas Longhorn. Other feral groups persist in small numbers in forest reserves.

> **Type:** feral taurine
> **Coat:** often black but various colors
> **Body:** small and slender
> **Horns:** varied, sometimes polled

Hawaiian Wild cows on Maui show a range of coat colors and patterns from their mixed ancestry. *John Orsbun, Shutterstock*

Hereford

The trademark of the Hereford is its white face, which the bulls stamp on all their progeny, whatever the breed of the cow. This famous beef breed originating on the borders of England and Wales has spread worldwide as a pure breed, as a terminal sire, and in numerous new breeds created by crossbreeding. The first Herefords arrived in the United States in 1816 or 1817, and a breed society was formed in 1881.

A breeding program to create a hornless Hereford in North America began in the early 1890s by introducing the polling factor from the Angus and the Red Poll, and a **Polled Hereford** breed society was formed in 1900. Another hornless line was created in Iowa by selecting for mutation within the breed; its herdbook was established in 1913. In England, a different route was chosen by making use of the polling factor in the Galloway to form the Poll Hereford.

The **Nellorford** in Brazil is a cross from Nelore bulls and Hereford cows. The **Herebu** in Argentina is in effect the **Braford**, a product of Brahman bulls mated with Hereford cows. The **Charford** in Arizona is 3/8 Hereford (the main component is Charolais) and a little Brahman. The **Victoria** in Texas is 3/4 Hereford and 1/4 Brahman and looks very like a Hereford. The Hereford was also used in creating the **Hays Converter** in Canada, and there are proportions of Hereford in several other new breeds.

A peaceful, matronly Hereford suckler cow is the ideal mother for beef calves.

Type: taurine
Uses: beef, terminal sire, suckler cows
Coat: red (dark to yellow-red), with white head, underside, and switch and often partial white dorsal line
Horns: middle length; also polled variety

Hérens

Type: taurine
Uses: dairy, beef, draft
Coat: dark red-brown to blackish-brown with faint red dorsal stripe
Horns: middle length and jaunty
Body: deep body, stocky, short legs, cows' average height 44 inches (112 cm)

This Swiss triple-purpose breed has had its own U.S. breed society since 1980 and is also in Canada's General Stud and Herdbook. It comes from central Valais, where it was one of the breeds used in the Battle of the Queens, an unusual Swiss festival in which cows go head-to-head in shoving matches. It is a small, stocky animal, with a hint of the Dexter about it—definitely Celtic in origin. There is an **Evolénard** variety, which has a coat ranging from red to black to dun, large areas of white on the under parts and legs, and a white dorsal stripe, but this variety is almost extinct.

Highland

The rugged Highland cattle of Scotland are eye-catching and instantly recognizable. They have long handlebar horns and a long, thick shaggy coat covering the face as well as the body. The coat can become very matted over the winter, with patches like felt, and the animal could almost be mistaken

Type: taurine
Uses: beef, also ornamental
Coat: long and thick, well insulated; usually red-brown but ranging from pale fawn and dun to black, also brindle
Horns: long handlebar, sweeping outward and curving at the tips

for a yak. The Highland is quite small in its native setting, where it looks right at home on the moors and mountainsides (and famously swimming across the straits from the islands to the mainland markets) and makes good lean beef out of not very much natural grazing. It grows larger in kinder environments and with better feeding.

Highland cattle first came into Canada in 1882 and into Montana and Wyoming in the early years of the twentieth century. In 1948, an American Scotch Highland Breeders' Association was formed to register purebred cattle; a Canadian society was formed in 1964. The breed has been used as a beef animal in northern states and as a sire on dairy cows to give lean beef and easier calving. It is also crossed with beef breeds for hybrid vigor, especially Hereford and also with the Beef Shorthorn. The latter cross

Above: Bred for the Scottish uplands, Highland cattle relish the snow and their shaggy coats provide excellent protection in bad weather.

Left: Long handlebar horns are a feature of Highland cattle.

has become established as the successful red-brown **Luing** beef breed, which was created between 1949 and 1965 by the Cadzow brothers in Argyll, and which has its own breed societies in the United Kingdom, the United States, Canada, Australia, and New Zealand.

Perhaps surprisingly, the Highland has found its way to warmer climates in countries such as Argentina and South Africa. There are probably about ten thousand Highland cattle in North America, and the ALBC lists it as "Recovering." Alternative names include Scotch Highland, Scottish Highland, West Highland, and Kyloe.

Hinterwald

Originating from the higher slopes of the southern Black Forest of Baden in Germany, this small Celtic type of cow is rare in its homeland and elsewhere. There has been a breed society in Germany since 1889, and one was formed in Switzerland a hundred years later. It was originally a triple-purpose breed but is now used for milk and meat. Lightly built, it is a yellow-pied breed and closely related to the red-pied **Vorderwald** found on the lower slopes in the central regions of the Black Forest. Both of these *Wäldervieh* ("forest cattle") types have white heads, chests, and under parts and often speckles of white on the body. Other names include Black Forest, Gelbscheck ("yellow pied"), Small Spotted Hill, and Scheckig ("pied").

Type: taurine
Uses: dairy, beef
Coat: yellow-and-white pied (Hinterwald), red-and-white pied (Vorderwald)
Body: small (especially Hinterwald), light dairy-type build
Horns: short

Hinterwald cows stand on a hillside in the Swiss Alps.

Holstein

The original home of what would become world-famous black-and-white milking cows was in the northern provinces of what is now The Netherlands, especially North Holland and Friesland.

In 1625, black-and-white Dutch cattle were brought to New Amsterdam. In 1852, a Dutch captain sold his ship's onboard milking Holland cow to a Massachusetts breeder, who was so impressed that he made further importations of this type over the next few years, and others joined him until an outbreak of disease in Europe halted all cattle imports.

The name of black-and-white Dutch dairy cows had a checkered history during their long period of export and expansion. There is no place called Holstein in The Netherlands, yet this country is the homeland of both the Holstein and the Friesian. The Dutch Black Pied (which itself has many synonyms) is the type from which the world's Friesian cattle were developed, and the world's Holstein cattle evolved from the Friesian. To cut a long and complicated story short, the "Holstein" originated from Dutch black-and-white cattle largely imported by Dutch settlers during the second half of the nineteenth century. Some of these imported cattle, though Dutch by birth, actually embarked from the northern German province of Schleswig-Holstein, on the Jutland peninsula; but the majority were shipped from Friesland or from North or South Holland. In America, the name "Holstein" stuck, even though 95 percent of the Dutch black-and-whites imported into North America for the half-century from 1852 had actually been bred in The Netherlands, especially Friesland, and not in Schleswig-Holstein.

By the 1860s, the Holstein-Friesian in North America had become established as a dairy breed based on cows from Holland, and in the latter part of the century,

The Holstein is the most prolific milk producer in the world, as shown by her large udder and the obvious "milk veins" that supply it.

various breed societies were formed, including a U.S. Holstein society in 1871 and a Dutch Friesian society in 1877. They merged in 1885, adopting the name of Holstein-Friesian, which since 1977 has usually been simplified to Holstein. Likewise, in Canada, the Holstein-Friesian breed society that formed in 1884 changed its name to Holstein one hundred years later. Since then, the Holstein cow has virtually taken over the dairy industry worldwide, with phenomenal milk yields.

Whereas the black-and-white was selectively bred for high milk yields in North America, in Europe the dual-purpose type, still called Friesian, was preferred as it could produce calves for the beef market as well as milk for the dairy sector. Hence the Friesian remained a sturdier beast altogether, and European breeders gently mocked the emerging longer-legged Holstein as a bony "coat hanger cow"—until they began to appreciate its productivity. Once the Holsteins began to infiltrate Europe, it did not take them long to overwhelm the traditional Friesian, which in some countries has fallen from being ubiquitous after World War II to being a minor breed and, in some places, almost a rare one.

There is a separately registered **Red-and-White Holstein** (or Red Holstein), identical in all except its color. In Colorado, an American Beef Friesian was developed from the traditional dual-purpose British Friesian. In some countries, attempts are being made to combine Holstein and Jersey to boost the solids content of Holstein milk; elsewhere, there is crossing with zebu cattle (but only a tiny proportion) to create a **Holstein Tropical** dairy breed. In Texas, the **Holgus** is a Holstein × Angus cross. But on the whole, the Holstein is simply valued for what she is: a superb producer of milk.

Type: taurine
Use: dairy
Coat: black-and-white pied (Holstein); red-and-white pied (Red-and-White Holstein)
Body: dairy conformation, large (long-legged)
Horns: short

Most Holsteins are black-and-white pied but there is a separate register for the Red-and-White.

Jamaican Breeds

The Ministry of Agriculture and local livestock farmers in Jamaica have successfully created new breeds as a nationwide joint venture, with all stages carefully documented. Full use has been made of the tropical adaptability of zebu cattle, which form the central core of the breeding programs. The **Jamaica Brahman** has a long history on the island. Indian zebu have been imported since 1860, and oxen of the Mysore breed were working in the sugar cane fields by the 1880s. Other Indian zebu breeds were grading and replacing the old creole cattle and put to work on banana plantations and elsewhere. An outbreak of foot-and-mouth disease precipitated by an importation of Nellore cows put a stop to all future imports direct from India, and the Jamaica Brahman was developed from the breeds already in the country.

The **Jamaica Hope** is a genuine tropical dairy breed based on a combination of the Jersey (the main proportion) and the Sahiwal zebu, with a small input from the Holstein. A breed society was formed in 1952. The cows are broadly similar to the Jersey in color and general appearance.

The polled **Jamaica Red** is based on the dual-purpose Red Poll from eastern England, which came to Jamaica in 1880 and adapted well there, with the addition of a little zebu blood by means of a South Devon/Indian zebu cross. The polled **Jamaica Black** is based on the Aberdeen-Angus, again with an infusion of zebu blood.

A young Jamaica Hope shows the strong Jersey influence. *R. J. Lerich, Shutterstock*

Jersey

The world-famous Jersey is easy to recognize, with its dark dished face, light mealy muzzle halo, long-lashed doe-like eyes, general daintiness, and attractive fawn-like calves. (There is an old fable that Jersey cattle are half-antelope!) The breed comes from the Channel Islands, and its impressive spread and success literally all over the world is all the more extraordinary when you consider that the British dependency of Jersey, just off the French coast, is so tiny. On the island, the breed was developed in isolation for two centuries after all cattle imports were banned in the eighteenth century. Above all, the Jersey is valued for the high butterfat content of its creamy milk, but also many love it simply for looking so decorative.

Jersey cattle probably first came to the United States in the 1850s, though there is much confusion about names for Channel Islands cattle; both Jersey and Guernsey were often referred to as Alderney cows, for example. A breed society was formed here in 1868—ten years before a society was formed in the United Kingdom. The Jersey is the epitome of a refined and elegant dairy type, slender in the legs, quite bony along the body (this is preferred by breeders, who want the cow's energy to go into her bag as milk, not on to her back as body fat), though the American Jersey has become rather larger and less graceful. There is also a **Polled Jersey**, for which a U.S. breed society was formed in 1895.

The Jersey's qualities have been taken into new breeds in other parts of the world such as the Australian Milking Zebu, the Jamaica Hope, the Jerdi in Brazil, the Jersind in India, the Nejdi in Iran and the Taylor in India, and have also been used to improve a few other breeds. Even without any zebu infusion, the Jersey has adapted happily to tropical environments and its genotype suggests some Iberian, Asian, and North African ancestry.

The coat coloring of the Jersey dairy cow is fairly similar to the Brown Swiss, but the Jersey has a much daintier build.

The typical "mealy" muzzle ring of the breed is shown on a Jersey. Look closely and you can see where the horns of this naturally short-horned breed would have sprouted if the farmer had not "disbudded" the cow as a calf.

Type: taurine
Use: dairy
Coat: usually fawn (typically soft tan), mulberry, or gray, but a wide range of colors possible (occasionally broken with white); often darker shading on face, hips, shoulders, legs, and switch; often with black skin and tongue
Horns: short
Body: light dairy conformation; smaller than Guernsey

Kerry

There is just a hint of the Jersey's elegance and carriage about the Kerry, a small, graceful black Celtic cow from Ireland that has gaily carried horns, an alert air, and a history that stretches back into ancient times. A reliable dairy breed, it makes a good family cow. As recently as the mid-nineteenth century, there was a red-eared white Kerry, though this color is no longer seen; red was common in the eighteenth century, and red calves are still born occasionally. There is a color-sided **Drimmond** variety. The much better-known little **Dexter** was developed from the Kerry.

The first Kerry cattle came to the United States in 1818 and for a century or so they prospered; there was a breed society from 1911 to 1921. But by the 1930s, they had almost disappeared, marginalized by more productive "improved" breeds to mountainous areas farmed by smallholders, and by the late 1980s there were none in the country at all. The Kerry is a very rare breed worldwide, even in Ireland; in the United States, it is on the ALBC "Critical" list and almost nonexistent, but there are a few in Canada and South Africa. What a waste of a beautiful and historic breed!

Type: taurine
Use: dairy
Coat: usually black, occasional small touches of white on underside
Horns: middle-length lyre
Body: light-boned dairy conformation; small

The Kerry milking cow has a very long history in Ireland but is now a rare breed at home and elsewhere.

Limousin

This is one of several beef breeds from central France that have made their mark in the United States in recent years, though the Limousin was earlier than most. It came into the country via Canada in the 1960s, and its American breed society was formed in 1969. It was originally a fast-moving draft animal in the Limoges area, but its breeders concentrated on meat production from the early twentieth century and it became one of France's two main beef breeds and beef sires for dairy herds. It has since been widely exported.

The **Brahmousin** in the southwestern states is based on Limousin bulls mated with Brahman cows; the breed is 3/8 Brahman, 5/8 Limousin. A Brahmousin breed society was established in 1984.

Type: taurine
Uses: beef
Coat: dark yellow-red shading to paler areas; also a black variety
Horns: middle length; also polled

France's Limousin has become widespread as a beef breed in recent years.

Lineback

The term lineback (also called finching, finchback, or rigget) means a white dorsal stripe, i.e. a sweep of white along the full length of the back of an otherwise dark-colored animal (usually red or black), and often includes sprinklings of white on the face, legs, and elsewhere. It is one stage of the color cline that ranges from color-pointed (white with colored extremities, especially ears and muzzle) to color-sided (white back, tail, and underside, with white or partly colored head and legs). These color patterns are seen in many European breeds and also in quite a few African ones.

In the American Lineback, there are two recognized patterns. One is the American "G" (for Gloucester), which has a base color of dark mahogany to black, with a white line along the back and over the tail and belly, very similar to (and possibly originating from) the Gloucester in England and the old Glamorgan in Wales. The other pattern is the Witrik, which has a color-sided coat that is red or black on the sides, with white along the back, belly, and lower legs, and white speckling on the face, possibly derived from the English Longhorn or the Dutch Witrik (*witrik* means "white back").

There is mention of a white-backed cow in the Plymouth Colony in 1627, which is hardly surprising considering the pattern was already common in several British and Dutch breeds. Thereafter, various European breeds that sometimes have a white dorsal line came into the United States—such as the Hereford, the old English Longhorn, and in particular a linebacked dark brown to black type of Holderness Shorthorn dairy cow. The latter was imported into New England from Yorkshire in the 1830s and came to be called the Columbian. By the early nineteenth century, Lineback was a recognized type of cattle seen in New England and was also found in Canada and in the Midwest.

In Vermont, local farmers formed a registry for American Lineback cattle in 1985, with one section for animals with the "G" pattern and another for the Witrik pattern. The latter are the most common today. Both types happen to have a lineback pattern, but there is not necessarily any direct relationship between them. Both types have probably received infusions of genes from various breeds over the years, including Shorthorn, Ayrshire, and Holstein. There is a lack of documentation that defies attempts to trace the real history of America's Linebacks.

For the Randall Lineback, see separate entry.

Type: taurine
Uses: dairy; or dual-purpose (dairy and beef)
Coat: red, brown, or black, with white back; some with white speckling on face
Horns: short

"Lineback" is a term that defines a coat pattern with white along the animal's back. The American Lineback has been bred for this pattern from various old European breeds. *J. Michael*

Maine-Anjou

A dual-purpose pied lowland breed from northwest France, the Maine-Anjou shows the influence of its Shorthorn ancestor in its coat color, which is red, roan, or red-and-white. It originated from Durham Shorthorn bulls crossed with Mancelle cows (it used to be called the Durham-Mancelle), and for a while it was combined with a similar but smaller French breed, the Armorican in northern Brittany, under the name of Rouge de l'Ouest ("western red"). It has been exported to Australasia and various European countries as well as North America and has had a U.S. breed society since 1969, when it first came into the country from Canada.

The **Brah-Maine** is 3/8 Brahman to 5/8 Maine-Anjou. A Brah-Maine breed society was established in 1985.

> **Type:** taurine
> **Uses:** beef, dairy
> **Coat:** red, red-and-white, or roan (usually dark red with small patches of white)
> **Body:** medium to large, quite long
> **Horns:** short

Marchigiana

A hardy upland breed that is popular in its native Italy, the Marchigiana, or Marky, is closely related to the Chianina, by which it was improved in the nineteenth century from a typical mountain Podolian type. It was also boosted by the Romagnola and has been classified as a pure breed in its own right since 1932. It has the Chianina's handsome markings: a white coat with black touches on the muzzle, switch, and around the eyes.

> **Type:** taurine
> **Use:** beef
> **Coat:** white with black points
> **Horns:** short to medium length, black tips

The touches of black highlight the pure white coat of the Italian Marchigiana.
Martie TenEyck, Marky Cattle Association

Mashona

Eastern Zimbabwe is the original home for these small, compact, tidy-looking sanga cattle that are used in Africa for draft work and as ranch beef animals. There is a grace and intelligence about them. In recent decades, they have been extensively crossed with European beef breeds and with the Africander, and there is now a stabilized humpless Mashona cross as well the humped sanga. Performance figures have been outstanding in its homeland for many years, where it has had a breed society since 1950. Local names include Shona, Makalanga, Makaranga, and Ngombe dza Vakaranga ("cattle of the Karanga").

Type: sanga
Use: beef
Coat: glossy, very short-haired; usually black, sometimes red, but also brown, brownish-black with lighter dorsal stripe, dun, yellow, cream, and various mottled and speckled mixtures and brindles
Horns: middle length, growing upward and outward; also often polled
Body: well-developed rounded muscular cervico-thoracic hump on bull (small on cow), also a humpless variety; small dewlap

A Mashona bull has a small sanga-type hump.

Meuse-Rhine-Yssel

This mouthful of a Netherlands breed is of the traditional dual-purpose type: meatier and more muscular than the neighboring black-and-whites but also a good yielder of milk with high protein content. Named for the three rivers (Meuse, Rhine, and Yssel) along which it originated, it absorbed several old red-pied breeds such as the Hollander, the Zeeland, the Drentish, and the Furnes-Ambacht. Other spellings and names for the breed include MRY, Maas-Rijn-Ijssel (MRI), Roodbont (meaning "red pied"), Dutch Red-and-White, and Red Pied Dutch. There is a darker-red variety, the **Brandrood**.

Type: taurine
Uses: dairy and meat (veal, beef)
Coat: red-and-white pied
Horns: short

Below: In The Netherlands, the sturdy Meuse-Rhine-Yssel is second only to the Dutch Black Pied as a dairy cow. It has contributed to the creation of several other red pied breeds in Europe, and its ancestral breeds (one of them similar to Scotland's Ayrshire) are often featured in old Dutch paintings. *Angela Diment, Woodland MRIs*

Miniature Cattle

On every continent in the Old World there are dwarf cattle, which measure up to 40 inches (100 cm) at the shoulder, but very few have been introduced into North America. The Dexter is one. However, some New World breeders have deliberately created miniature cattle, usually for their novelty value and sometimes for use in laboratory work. There is a **Miniature Galloway** in Australia, a **Miniature Hereford** in Texas bred selectively for small size by Rust Largent, a **Miniature Zebu** (or Mini Zebu) less than 42 inches tall with its own U.S. breed society since 1991, and a **Bonsai Zebu** (or Bonsai Brahman or Mini-Brahman) in Mexico bred selectively for small size from the Indo-Brazilian zebu since 1970 at the National Autonomous University and generally about 40 inches (100 cm) tall. In Columbia, Missouri, there is a line of miniature zebu cattle that apparently have "phenotypical similarities to laron dwarfism."

Then there is a whole host of miniature breeds originating at the Happy Mountain Miniature Cattle Farm, including trademark names like Panda®, Belted Irish Jersey®, Belted Milking Dexter®, American Beltie®, Mini Holstein®, Barbee®, Five Breed Grad-Wohl®, and so on. Only time will tell whether these breeding programs are successful and useful. The farm has also registered an International Miniature Cattle Breeders Society in Covington, Washington.

The Panda® is one of many new small breeds created at the Happy Mountain Miniature Cattle Farm in Covington, Washington. The reason for this little one's name is obvious; the panda-like facial markings complement the white belt. *Richard Gradwohl*

Murray Grey

Australia is the home of several breeds that have found, or could find, their way into the United States, and the Murray Grey has had a U.S. breed society since 1969. It entered the country as semen from Australia. The breed originated in the Upper Murray river valley in the state of Victoria, southeast Australia, and it all began in 1905 when an almost-white roan Shorthorn cow bred to a black Angus bull began to produce a series of gray calves. Thereafter, the breeder continued to grade to the Angus, selecting for gray or dun, until the new gray breed was stabilized. The color and the Angus's polling factor are dominant. A breed society was eventually formed in 1962, and the gentle, docile Murray Grey became popular both in Australia and overseas. In North America, it has succeeded in climates that range from tropical to the snowline.

Type: taurine
Use: beef
Coat: silver to dark gray, or gray dun
Horns: polled

Below: This Australian breed's ancestral near-white Shorthorn cow gave birth to a series of unusual silver calves at Thologolong Station, near Wodonga, Victoria, a century ago.

New American Breeds

The cocktail brewing of new breeds from mixtures of existing ones continues apace in the United States, as well as in Canada and Australia and elsewhere. Some may stabilize as true breeds; some are no more than hybrids and crosses. Some of the zebu crosses are discussed in the Brahman section, but there are many more combinations that use only humpless taurine breeds.

In New Mexico, the **Beef Machine** is a combination of Red Poll, Hereford, Brown Swiss, Angus, Friesian, and Simmental; while in North Dakota at the Cedar Ridge Ranch the **Better Idea** was achieved by putting Angus bulls on cross-bred females from matings between Brown Swiss and Hereford. In Nebraska, the **Cuprem Hybrid** was devised by A. Mulford of Kenesaw between 1960 and 1976 from a complicated mixture of half a dozen breeds. The dams were a mixture of Red Angus (1/2), Santa Gertrudis (1/4), and Limousin (1/4), and the sires were a mixture of Shorthorn (1/2), Charolais (1/4), and Chianina (1/4). The **Magnum** is a commercial hybrid in Iowa, which is also the home of the **RX3** (Red Angus, Hereford, and Red Holstein), and its own breed society formed in 1974. The **MARC** series developed in Nebraska at the eponymous Meat Animal Research Center has included numerous different breeds in different mixtures involving, for example, Angus, Braunvieh, Charolais, Gelbvieh, Hereford, Limousin, Pinzgauer, Red Poll, and Simmental. There

are many more mixtures, but it will take years before it is known which of them is useful and lasting.

On the western ranges from which it takes its name, the **Ranger** had a complicated history. This beef breed originated in 1970 by combining the **Hash Cross** with cattle from the Ritchie herd in Wyoming and the Watson herd in California. This bloodline involves a lot of different breeds, so concentrate.

First, the Hash Cross. The name is an acronym: HASH stands for Highland, Angus, Shorthorn, Hereford. It was created by E. and F. Barnes in Wyoming and is based on a Milking Shorthorn × Hereford, crossed with Red Angus bulls and later Highland bulls, and in a separate line it also used the Beefmaker.

The Ritchie herd put Brahman crossbred cows to bulls of several breeds: Simmental, Hash Cross, Beefmaster, Hereford, Brahman, and Highland × Shorthorn. Are you still following this? Meanwhile, the Watson herd put Hereford cows to bulls of the following breeds: American Brown Swiss, Red Angus × Red Holstein, Beefmaster, Hash Cross, and assorted dairy-breed bulls.

The Ranger is the product of mixing all these bloodlines. So now you know. The bulls varied considerably but at least the cow side of things is quite simple— mostly Hereford. The resulting offspring are as mixed as the parentage.

Normandy

The Normandy, or Norman, cow is known in its French homeland as the Normande. It is a dual-purpose (milk and meat) breed and quite unusual in its coat pattern, which is reminiscent of an abstract painting, as if the artist has dabbed random small splotches of reddish-brown and black over a white canvas, the splotches and spots sometimes merging into large patches and brindles and sometimes looking like impressionist flowers on the dished face and around the eyes (the breed usually has "spectacles" of color ringing the eyes). It is one of France's largest breeds, and in Norman times, it served as a monastic draft ox on the Channel Islands of Guernsey and Alderney. There is something Scandinavian about it, and indeed it might well have Viking origins. In the nineteenth century, it was crossed with the Durham Shorthorn and the Channel Islands cattle, which probably accounts for its useful meatiness and the high butterfat levels in its milk (the source of Camembert cheese). It found its way into the United States, where a breed society was formed in 1974.

Type: taurine
Uses: dairy, beef
Coat: tricolored (flaxen, white, and brindle), usually dark reddish brown and black scattered on white, with colored eye rings
Body: large and well fleshed, with large chest and pelvis
Horns: short

The coat pattern on the large old French Normandy cow is eye-catching.

Parthenais

In Deux-Sèvres, western France, this old yellow-brown breed in the Poitou region used to number three-quarters of a million animals before World War II, but after the war it declined rapidly, crashing to about 20,000 by 1980. It started out as a triple-purpose breed, especially for work and meat, with milk of lesser importance, but increasingly became a beef breed. It bears a resemblance to the neighboring Limousin but has a black muzzle and is larger. Its range of names includes Choletais, Gâtinais, Gâtine(lle), and

Vendée-Parthenay. Varieties include the **Nantais** (a paler variety, with a brown to silver-gray coat and without the black muzzle; it is a dual-purpose type for dairy and beef) and the **Maraîchin** (with a brown or yellow coat and lyre-shaped horns; originally a triple-purpose type but now mainly beef).

Type: taurine
Use: mostly beef
Coat: fawn, with dark muzzle
Body: large
Horns: middle length

Piedmontese

An interesting breed that is difficult to categorize, this is a fairly tall gray-brown animal of the plains of northern Italy. Once triple-purpose, it has been strongly selected for

Type: taurine
Use: beef, sire on dairy cows
Coat: white to pale gray or light gray-brown, with black switch, muzzle, hooves, and ears
Body: tall; fine boned, double-muscled
Horns: short

beef in recent years and now tends to be double-muscled like the Belgian Blue.

The Piedmontese (or Piedmont) became popular in The Netherlands as a beef sire on dairy farms and it seems to "nick" (combine well genetically in crossbreeding programs) with Holstein cows. A U.S. breed society was formed in 1984.

The **Tarentaise** comes from the same region. Up in the French Alps, this hardy dual-purpose local breed was nearly obliterated in the late nineteenth century in a pincer movement from the neighboring Piedmontese beef cattle and good red milking cows from Bergamo. It survived, though, and by 1979 it numbered 150,000 in France. Breed societies were formed in the United States and Canada by 1973, and also in Australia. In the Alps, there are two types: a smaller one in the mountains and, naturally, a larger one in the valleys. It remains a milk-and-meat breed. It is known in Italy as the Tarina.

The Piedmontese is usually a pale brownish-gray and is more closely linked to breeds of the northern Italian plains than to the gray-white Podolian breeds such as the Chianina and Marchigiana.

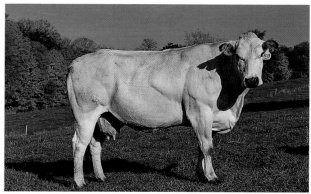

Pinzgauer

An attractively marked Austrian linebacked breed, the Pinzgauer wears immediately recognizable garter-like white leg "britches" set against its rich mahogany coat. Its clean white finchback continues on the tail and along the underside as well. It is essentially a dual-purpose breed, for meat and milk. It is related to the Hérens, among others, and reached a peak of popularity in the nineteenth-century glory days of the Austro-Hungarian empire. Surprisingly, it was successfully exported to what was then the German colony of South West Africa (now Namibia) as early as 1900 and remains there today. It has spread to many other countries, and a U.S. breed society was formed in 1973. There is a polled **Jochberg** variety. The **Pinzbrau** is a U.S. cross of Pinzgauer bulls on Brown Swiss cows.

Type: taurine
Uses: dairy, beef
Coat: color-sided (red-brown and white) with colored head
Horns: short

An old Alpine breed, the Pinzgauer is a good and long-lived suckler cow.

The dramatic coat pattern of the Pinzgauer includes its white "britches," not usually seen in other lineback breeds.

Randall Blue Lineback

Type: taurine
Uses: dairy, beef, draft
Coat: brockled blue-black sides, white back and underside
Horns: middle length in larger dairy type; short in smaller dairy type and in small dual-purpose type

This interesting closed dairy herd of linebacked cattle has been maintained by the Randall family in Arlington, Vermont, for some eighty years and is known to have included some Guernsey blood in the early years from the family's milking herd. The entire herd was dispersed in 1985, but fortunately most of them were gathered together by sympathetic breeders rather than slaughtered. Blood-typing has been carried out and shows that the herd is distinct from other dairy breeds. It is of Dutch origin with the addition of English, Channel Islands, or Breton and possibly Scandinavian cattle. These animals are now described as a "landrace" breed by the ALBC (i.e. a local population that has enough consistency to be considered a breed but that has more variability than found within standard breeds) and have officially been named the Randall Blue Lineback. A careful breeding program is in place, the largest herd now being in Tennessee.

The Randall Blue's color pattern is its most defining feature. The breed is color-sided, originally having a black or blue-black coat with white spotting called "brockling" that produces an effect similar to roan; it has the classic white back, and the rest of the body is white apart from dark, often brockled, muzzle, ears, and eye rings. Different

The color-sided coat pattern of the Randall Blue is often seen in Scandinavian breeds and also in the Vosges (a mountain breed of the Alsace region related to Germany's Black Forest cattle).

types are beginning to emerge within the breed, including dairy and dual-purpose (both small and larger) conformations, and colors such as mahogany, gray, and red. The ALBC status for the Randall Blue is "Critical," but the numbers have increased tenfold in the past twenty years, and they are being used, largely by small-scale farmers, for

Just good friends—an enchanting pair of Randall Blue calves.

Red Dane

The Danish Red, known in the United States as the American Red Dane, originated in Denmark (where it was first recognized as a breed in 1878) as a dairy cow of the Baltic Red type. Since 1975, it has been improved in Denmark with the help of American Brown Swiss blood and other breeds; the purebred old type is re-

> **Type:** taurine
> **Use:** dairy
> **Coat:** deep red
> **Horns:** short

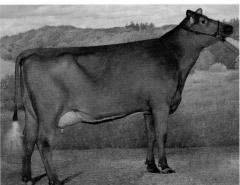

tained as a dual-purpose (milk and beef) breed in the breeding group known as the RDM-1970 (the initials stand for Rødt Dansk Malkekvaeg, or Red Danish Milking Cow). The U.S. herdbook opened in 1948.

Denmark's red dairy cow is similar to other Baltic red cattle but more carefully bred. *Elly Geverink, Dansire International*

Red Poll

One cannot help having a soft spot for this fine East Anglian breed, which used to be one of England's most popular and reliable dual-purpose cows, giving beefy calves as well as serving as

Type: taurine
Uses: beef, originally also dairy
Coat: rich red; skin pigmented
Horns: polled
Body: medium size, deep bodied

a dairy cow. It originated early in the nineteenth century from two once-famous breeds: the small, meaty Devon-like Norfolk Red and the big, milky hornless Suffolk Dun. The latter looked exactly like a yellow version of the Galloway.

Cattle of both the Norfolk and the Suffolk types came into North America with early settlers, and several hundred registered Red Polls were imported mainly in the 1870s and 1880s. The U.S. breed society was formed in 1883, and one formed in 1905 in Canada, where it is often called a mooly or a muley, meaning "hornless." It became popular in both countries, with substantial numbers registered on both sides of the border in the 1950s.

By the 1960s, it was promoted as a beef breed rather than dual-purpose, and it officially became a beef breed in the United States in 1972; by the late 1980s, there was only one milking herd left in the country.

The popularity of the beef type waned and it is now listed by the ALBC as "Threatened" in the United States. In its homeland, where it remained largely a dual-purpose type, it is also rare, but in the meantime it has been widely exported, especially to South America, Australasia, and Africa. And its useful sun-proof pigmented skin and the polling factor have contributed to the creation of new tropical breeds such as the Senepol in the U.S. Virgin Islands, the Jamaica Red, the Pitangueiras in Brazil, and the La Velasquez in Colombia.

The Red Poll is valued for its sun-proof red coat, its natural lack of horns, and its motherliness.

Romagnola

One of Italy's gray-white Podolian group of cattle (which includes the Chianina), this robust breed used to be widespread in its home region of Emilia Romagna. Its population in Italy has dropped sharply since World War II. Originally valued as a working animal, it is now a beef breed and was improved before 1900 with the help of the Chianina and the Reggiana (an old dark yellow, dual-purpose Italian breed). The coat of the Romagnola is white in summer, gray in winter (it can grow long and thick in wet conditions), shading to darker areas. The skin is pigmented. Calves are born a tan color. It is well established in North America and has had breed societies in the United States and Canada since 1974. The **Romangus** is a combination of Romagnola with Angus.

Type: taurine
Use: beef
Coat: light gray to white; skin pigmented
Horns: middle to long lyre-shaped
Body: can be heavy-boned

Calves of the Romagnola and other Podolian breeds, such as Chianina and Marchigiana, are usually born with red or yellow coats, gradually changing to gray or white as they grow.

Romosinuano

Type: taurine
Use: beef
Coat: red
Horns: polled

In Colombia, some useful breeds are based on criollo cattle, and this is one of them. It was bred for beef in a closed herd at Turipana (near Cerete, in Cordoba), and its particular features are a red coat and a polled head, both of which have probably been influenced by the Red Poll and Red Angus. From the Romosinuano another breed was created. The polled red beef **La Velasquez** was bred on the Hacienda Africa at La Dorada, Caldas, from Red Poll bulls and crossbred zebu/Romosinuano cows. (There are several other interesting Colombian criollo-based breeds, including the color-pointed Blanco Orejinegro, which has a white coat over pigmented skin, and black ears and muzzle—a color type that is seen quite often in criollo cattle.)

The light dewlap on this bull suggests some zebu blood. Crossbred zebu/Romosinuano cows have been bred to Red Poll bulls to create a polled La Velasquez beef breed.

Also known as the Polled Sinú, named for the Sinú River on the humid Caribbean coastal plains of Colombia, the Romosinuano has a horned relative (Costeño con Cuernos) that displays typical spreading criollo horns.

Salers

Type: taurine
Uses: beef and dairy; good suckler cow
Coat: deep chestnut, also black
Horns: long, growing outward and then curving up, back, and out; also polled
Body: large for a mountain breed

All over France's Massif Central in May, the beef herds would be moved up to high grazings in a tradition known as *l'estive*, which always called for celebrations and festivities. The handsome chestnut-red Salers cattle of Cantal, Auvergne, would be decorated with tricolor ribbons around their long elegantly curving horns and would walk along town and village main streets, cowbells clanging and calves at foot, while bands played.

The Salers (note that the final "s" is part of the name—it is not a plural) has been recognized since 1853 as a breed. It is a hardy mountain animal whose curly coat protects it against cold, wet weather, but in hotter conditions the coat becomes smooth and sleek, and its pigmented skin protects it from the sun. It has swapped genes both ways in the past two centuries with England's red Devon; it was also boosted with some Shorthorn and Highland blood in the nineteenth century, and today is sometimes crossed with the Charolais. The Salers first came into the United States in the early 1970s, and there have been American and Canadian breed societies since 1974.

The **Salorn** has been developed in Texas since the 1980s by mating Salers and Texas Longhorn, the final proportion being 5/8 Salers; it was recognized as a breed in 1986. The **Salerford** is simply a crossbreed resulting from using a Salers bull on a Hereford cow.

The **Bralers** is 5/8 Salers and 3/8 Brahman. The usual and preferred color is solid red, but on bulls there may be some black shading on the rump and shoulders. A Bralers breed society was established in 1984, at a time when many new Brahman-based breeds were being formalized. A wave of new European breeds began to enter the United States from Canada in the 1960s, and breeders were quick to adapt them by all possible means, including crossbreeding, to local situations.

In its native France, the fine old Salers cow has a wonderfully deep mahogany coat and quite dramatic horns. The trend in the United States is for a black coat and no horns.

Santa Gertrudis

The creation of this big and hugely successful red Texan beef breed is wrapped up in the story of the famous King Ranch (see chapter 1).

In about 1910, the ranch received a half-Brahman bull, which was mated with Shorthorn cows. One of the offspring, a red bull named Chemmera, was also put with the Shorthorn cows, and the offspring from both bulls were interesting enough to encourage the ranch to acquire a large number of part-bred Brahman bulls (no purebred ones being available) and continue the experiment. One of the bulls was mated to a cow that already had 1/16 Brahman blood from Chemmera, and her cherry-red calf from this mating would become the foundation sire for the new Santa Gertrudis breed; he was called Monkey (for his playfulness) and lived from 1919 until 1932, and all Santa Gertrudis cattle today are descended from him. The breed was formally recognized as pure in 1940, and a breed society was formed in 1951. At present, the proportions within the breed are about 5/8 Shorthorn and 3/8 Brahman, and the accepted coat color is a deep cherry-red. It is named after the original land purchased by the founder of the King Ranch, Captain Richard King. The breed has been exported widely and has breed societies or herdbooks in several Latin American countries, Canada, Australia, New Zealand, South Africa, and Russia.

> **Type:** zebu/taurine composite
> **Use:** beef
> **Coat:** solid cherry-red (light to dark); skin red pigmented
> **Horns:** short, or polled
> **Body:** deep, strong-boned; medium to large ears slightly drooping

The long semi-lop ears of the Santa Gertrudis are proof of its part-zebu ancestry.

Senepol

Type: taurine
Uses: dairy, beef
Coat: red; skin pigmented, red to black
Horns: polled

It is unusual for humpless (i.e. neither zebu nor sanga) native African breeds to be used in an American context, but the doughty small **N'Dama** of Guinea and neighboring West African countries has considerable potential and has been put to good use in the U.S. Virgin Islands, on St Croix, to create the Senepol.

In its own region, the N'Dama shares with other native West African breeds a high degree of resistance (called trypanotolerance) to trypanosomiasis, a disease caused by protozoan parasites and transmitted by the bite of tsetse flies. The N'Dama is unusual in West Africa for having long rather than short horns and for its good potential for beef. It is compact, with short legs, and its coat is generally yellow to light red (the color range includes pied and even color-pointed white), with pigmented sunproof skin

N'Dama Petite cattle were exported from Senegal to the West Indies (Martinique and Guadeloupe) as early as the mid-nineteenth century. In 1860, N'Dama cattle were imported for the Nelthropp herd in St Croix.

The Senepol was created from N'Dama cows bred to Red Poll bulls between 1918 and 1949. A polled red dual-purpose breed, the Senepol (*Sene* for Senegal, *pol* for the Red Poll) is well suited to its tropical environment. A breed society was formed in 1976.

The compact, well-built beef frame of the ancestral N'Dama can be seen in the Senepol.

The Senepol of the West Indies developed from an unusual combination of a West African humpless longhorn breed and England's Red Poll.

Shorthorn

The Shorthorns are historically important British cattle, not only in their homeland but worldwide. They were already known in England in the sixteenth century, and by the eighteenth, they were usually called simply the "Dutch breed," found on the east coast. Their long and interesting story has been told in several books and embraces famous old Shorthorn cattle types such as the Teeswater and the Durham. The first herdbook in the world was published privately by George Coates in 1822 for Shorthorns.

Type: taurine
Uses: beef, dairy
Coat: roan, red, or white; also red-and-white, roan-and-white
Horns: short; also polled

In the eighteenth century, the most important breed in Britain was the **English Longhorn**, developed by the famous breeder Robert Bakewell of Dishley, Leicestershire, the first of the great improvers, who perfected a system of inbreeding and ruthless culling and knew exactly what he wanted from his breed. But his hugely commercial improved Longhorn (which, incidentally, was exported to the United

The dramatically long horns of the old English Longhorn can grow in various directions and remain a strong feature of the breed today. It is not related to or influenced by the Texas Longhorn.

States after the American Revolution but is no relation of the Texas Longhorn, though it has equally dramatic horns) would be totally eclipsed by the Shorthorn group in the nineteenth century.

In Britain, the Shorthorns gradually divided into different types. In Scotland, they became a **Beef Shorthorn**, while in northeast England they became a dual-purpose **Dairy Shorthorn**, and there were also strains or minor separate breeds such as the **Northern Dairy Shorthorn**, the **Whitebred Shorthorn**, and initially the **Lincoln Red**.

Both the beef and the dual-purpose types of Shorthorn have been exported all over the world and have often been used to improve other breeds or create new ones (the list is very long and at least thirty breeds in the United States today have Shorthorn blood).

Roan is a typical coat color in the various Shorthorn breeds, including this Beef Shorthorn cow.

Shorthorns of various types and under various names followed the Longhorn into the United States. In 1783, for example, "Milk Breed" or "Durham" Shorthorns arrived in Virginia. Over the next few decades, there were many Shorthorn importations; these useful animals not only provided milk and beef but also made good working oxen. The cattle spread out to the Midwest, finding their way to the other side of the

Mississippi by 1839, when they reached Missouri. They were particularly popular in Shaker communities. An American Shorthorn herdbook was first published in 1846, and in 1882, a combined breed association for both an American "Milking Shorthorn" and a "Scotch" or Scottish (beef) Shorthorn was formed. There was a growing color prejudice against the roan that is typical of many Shorthorns; American breeders preferred solid red (as they had shown in their liking for the Devon and the Hereford, for example), and no doubt some valuable genotypes were lost in selecting for color.

In the early years of the twentieth century, with the increasing emphasis on beef production, the milkiness of the old dual-purpose Shorthorn was being ignored. Recognizing the risk, several breeders began to select for milkiness and, in 1948, formed a separate society for the **Milking Shorthorn**. In 1969, the American Milking Shorthorn was formally declared a breed and was increasingly developed as a dairy type. Today it is on the ALBC "Watch" list.

Meanwhile, the beefier Shorthorns, known simply as the **American Shorthorn**, surged on across the continent and became an essential part of ranching in both North and South America. A **Polled Shorthorn** or "Polled Durham" was developed in Ohio for beef, originating from a mutation—rather than crossing with a polled breed—in the late nineteenth century. The **Brahorn** is a first cross from Brahman bulls on Shorthorn cows for beef.

Back home in Britain, the Beef Shorthorn became a rare breed, and the dual-purpose Dairy Shorthorn quickly lost its dominant place to the British Friesian and the Holstein.

These Milking Shorthorn cows show some of the other coat colors and patterns seen in Shorthorns.

Simmental

Switzerland's Simme valley was the home of an old pied breed known as the Bernese: sometimes blond red-and-white, sometimes solid red, sometimes black-and-white. These cattle lived in mixed herds, but during the nineteenth century, the black-and-whites, which tended to be taller and more robust, were separated from the rest. The red-and-whites would become the Simmental, a triple-purpose type whose breeders preferred a yellowish-red pied coat and a white face, legs, and tail. The first small U.S. herd was established in Texas in 1886, and almost immediately Americans were buying Simmentals at the rate of three to every two Swiss Brown that they purchased. Yet it was not until the early 1960s that Simmental numbers really began to grow fast, with semen importations from Germany, Switzerland, and France. U.S. and Canadian breed societies were formed in 1968 and 1969.

> **Type:** taurine
> **Uses:** beef, dairy
> **Coat:** dun-red and white, or yellow-leather and white; white face
> **Horns:** short

A blockier type was soon developed in which the originally excellent milk-producing qualities were unimportant. Then it was decided to bolster milk production in the breed in Switzerland by introducing plenty of Red Holstein blood in the 1960s (though four decades later the Swiss animal is increasingly beefy).

Meanwhile Simmentals had been widely exported and developed in different ways in different parts of the world, improving local cattle and often contributing to new breeds. In the United States, for example, there is the large red **Simbrah** (with white markings), having 1/2 to 3/4 Simmental blood and the remainder Brahman, which was known as the Brahmental until 1978. Mel Lauriton developed the **Simmalo** in California. The mix is 1/2 Simmental, 1/4 Hereford, and 1/4 bison. The **Simbrangerford** is a combination of Simmental, Brangus, and Hereford. Several countries have developed other combinations, such as the **Simford** (Simmental and Hereford), which has a deep honey to red coat with a white face. Like the Hereford, the Simmental's trademark white face is passed to any offspring of a Simmental bull

Other names for the Simmental include Swiss Red Spotted and Fleckvieh (a German name meaning "pied cattle").

A Simmental cow in her native Switzerland has been allowed to grow her horns.

South Devon

Although originally from the same southwest English county as the beefy "Ruby Red" Devon and the Milking Devon, there is something different about the South Devon. It is much

> **Type:** taurine
> **Use:** beef, originally also dairy
> **Coat:** light red to yellow-red
> **Body:** larger than other British breeds
> **Horns:** short

bigger (once the biggest in Britain) and more yellow than its neighbor. Factors in its hemoglobin link it to the dairy cattle of the Channel Islands and, like them, to Asian cattle and some of the African ones as well. Blood-typing studies in the 1980s also revealed that, genetically, it was even closer to the yellow Gelbvieh of central Germany and the Swiss Brown than it was to, say, England's Hereford, though it also has a close affinity with the Hereford and the north Devon.

It used to be a dual-purpose breed, with quite a few dairy herds in its home area where its milk provided the famous Devon clotted cream. But a decision was made by English breeders to forget about milk and concentrate on beef; since 1972, it has been classified as a beef breed.

In England, the South Devon was largely confined to southern Devon, particularly the area known as the South Hams (the breed is also known as the "Hammer" and the "Big Red"), but it has been widely exported to North and South America, Australia, and New Zealand and also to South Africa, where it has been particularly successful and is often used in crossbreeding with Brahman and Africander cows. Breed societies were formed in the United States and Canada in 1974.

The **South Bravon** is the cross between Brahman bulls and South Devon cows.

Sometimes known as the "Big Red" in England, the South Devon is more yellow than the neighboring "Ruby Red" of north Devon.

Sussex

There are several red English breeds, all originally triple-purpose animals that worked on the land as well as giving meat and milk, and the Sussex of southern England was a particularly useful draft ox.

Type: taurine
Use: beef
Coat: dark rich red, white switch
Horns: middle length

It is a good solid type, makes good beef, and has an interesting habit of indiscriminate grazing. It will munch its way across the pasture like a vacuum cleaner, not fussy about what it eats and not leaving ragged clumps of coarse grasses and weeds.

Its very deep red color has helped it to gain popularity in hot climates—and it also has twice as many sweat glands as other European breeds, putting it on par with the Africander. It has been exported to countries such as South Africa (where a **Polled Sussex** has been formed with the aid of polled Red Angus bulls), Zambia, and New Zealand. It has long been established in the United States, where a breed society was first formed as early as 1884, but numbers were never high, though fresh importations after World War II increased the population and a new American association was formed in 1966. The red **Sabre** beef breed originated from 1950 onward in Texas at the Lambert ranch, Refugio, from Sussex bulls crossed with Brahman cows, the final proportion being 7/8 Sussex.

A Sussex cow is happy to raise two calves together, and she is capable of giving birth to her first calf when she is only two years old. Her white switch is typical of the breed.
Chris Capstick, Lower Roundhurst Farm

Texas Longhorn

There are many romantic tales about this movie-classic but increasingly rare breed. It is basically a Spanish criollo, first imported in the mid-seventeenth century probably as Andalusians.

The Texas Longhorn is perhaps one of the most romanticized remnants of the old Spanish cattle. It can trace its history to a herd of criollo driven north through Mexico to the Sabine River in 1690. By 1860, there were millions of feral criollo in Texas, unbranded, unowned, fending for themselves quite happily and reproducing prolifically. It was after the Civil War that criollo began to be rounded up on a large scale and driven to the railheads for transportation to the cities of the north—and this was the height of the cowboy period made famous on the screen. In truth, those exciting days of massive herds being headed up and moved on in galloping clouds of dust by whooping men with lariats across the wide open spaces really lasted only twenty years or so. At its peak in 1870, there were probably some 40 million cattle in Texas, most of them Longhorns. But by the end of that century, the Longhorn would be almost extinct.

J. Frank Dobie tells the story at length in his book *The Longhorns* (1941), laced with legends of cowboys, stampedes, battling bulls, epic treks, and a lot more besides, some of it just a little bit fanciful. But unquestionably the Longhorn played a major role in the days when herds of several thousand animals were driven for more than a

A Texas Longhorn cow in Texas Hill Country sports the breed's classic horns.

A Texas Longhorn bull has an interesting color-sided coat pattern. Unusually, he has the white "britches" seen in the Pinzgauer. There is a very wide range of coat colors and patterns in criollo cattle.

thousand miles from the Texas ranges to the railheads and markets, where they could be sold for ten times the price they would fetch in Texas. Some 10 million Texan cattle had made such journeys before the end of the nineteenth century. On one occasion in 1869, a massive 15,000 head formed a single drive; on another in 1854, the first Longhorns to reach New York City took a year to cover the ground. These range cattle required good legs, the stamina to endure the journey and remain calm enough not to stampede along the way, and the ability to withstand difficult environments and diseases and pests—and, at the end of day, still make beef.

From being almost uncountably high, numbers of the pure Longhorn began to falter from crossbreeding as the nineteenth century progressed, especially to imported British cattle such as Shorthorn, Angus, and Hereford. By the turn of that century, the majority of American beef cattle contained some Longhorn blood, but it was not long before beef farmers and ranchers preferred the British breeds instead of the Longhorn and also began using the Brahman in the hotter regions. In addition, the open ranges that had so suited the breed became fenced. Ranching methods were changing, and the Longhorn—already a problem precisely because of its darned long horns (try loading that lot into cattle wagons!)—was fighting a losing battle in these new times.

In 1927, the government realized it had to take steps to prevent the actual extinction of the true Texas Longhorn. A preservation herd—three bulls and twenty cows—was established in Oklahoma at the Wichita Mountains Wildlife Refuge, and later another small herd was established in Nebraska. Just in time. By 1960, there were only about 1,500 pure Longhorns left in the country and the numbers were still falling when the Texas Longhorn Breeders' Association was formed in 1964.

But it takes a lot to destroy the Longhorn! Its population has grown rapidly since then, and with its inherent qualities once again being appreciated, there are now some 100,000 registered animals in the breed. There are also still Longhorns in Canada. They were first brought into Alberta in 1876. Impressively, the Texas Longhorn is no longer an endangered breed.

Type: taurine
Uses: beef, rodeo
Coat: wide range of colors (red most common) and patterns
Horns: long handlebar
Body: elliptical, long-legged

A Longhorn displays another good example of those handlebar horns.

The **Texon** is an attempt to create a new breed, since 1989, by crossing Devon bulls on the Texas Longhorn; the **Salorn** is based on a more complicated crossing with Salers bulls; the **Geltex** uses Gelbvieh bulls; and no doubt there is a Texbrah or Brahtex on the horizon.

The Texas Longhorn is instantly recognizable by its dramatic, wide-sweeping handlebar horns, which are also seen in the Spanish cattle from which it is descended. There is a distance of at least 40 inches (100 cm) between the tips, and some individuals have had a horn span that stretched as much as 9 feet (2.7 m). There were fanciful claims at one time that the breed owed its horns to the old English Longhorn, and even as recently as 1973 it was stated firmly by one source that "the Texas Longhorn was the result of crossing the Mexican fighting bulls with English-bred Longhorns which were regularly shipped out of Liverpool along with the human migrants throughout the 19th century." There is absolutely no substance to such a notion, any more than there would be in a claim that this great range animal got its horns from Africa. The Texas Longhorn is a Spaniard, albeit by way of Mexico.

Fortunately for the cows, it takes a while for a Longhorn calf's horns to develop!

Tuli

In southwest Zimbabwe, the Tuli sanga has been carefully selected for a golden-brown coat from the Amabowe variety of the native Tswana since 1946 (when the country was known as Rhodesia and was a major beef producer constantly experimenting with an assortment of sanga, zebu, and European breeds); its breed society was formed in 1961. Farmer Len Harvey initially collected the Amabowe animals, hence the Tuli is sometimes known as "Harvey's cattle." He was lucky to find them: 95 percent of the Mangwato cattle had been wiped out by cattle plague by 1896.

Some of the Tswana cattle are naturally polled; others have long horns—sometimes very long—and a wide range of coat colors and patterns. All of them are basically good beef animals, and there is a **Botswana Beef Synthetic** that combines Tswana, Tuli, American Brahman (zebu), Bonsmara from South Africa (sanga/taurine mixture of Africander, Shorthorn, and Hereford), and Simmental.

Type: sanga
Use: beef
Coat: golden brown, yellow or red
Horns: long, or polled

Below: There is good beef potential in the Tuli, a golden-brown breed developed in Zimbabwe.

Wagyu

Type: taurine
Use: beef
Coat: black or reddish-brown
Horns: short

The **American Wagyu** was formed in Texas from a combination of two Japanese breeds (Japanese Black and Japanese Brown) with Hereford and Angus. The word *wagyu* means "native Japanese cattle."

Japan does not have a long tradition of cattle breeding. It is largely an arable nation, and animal protein is consumed mainly from fish rather than farm livestock. The land is too densely populated to allow extensive grazing. In fact, it was not until the nineteenth century, after a thousand years of Buddhist (and Shinto) restrictions, that any public demand was made for meat and milk. Livestock until that time were used only for work and for their manure. There were no indigenous Japanese breeds, but cattle were imported from the Asian continent and, because of Japanese isolationism and bans on foreign trade for two centuries up to 1854, they did develop into recognizable native types called Wagyu. But after the reforms of 1868, westernization was suddenly encouraged, including livestock imports, and there was so much crossbreeding with the imported breeds that purebred native Wagyu rapidly became rare. Today, the demand for high-quality beef is strong in Japan, and a high percentage of the beef breeds are based on Wagyu that were improved from the early twentieth century with the help of imported British and Continental breeds.

The **Japanese Native** breed is the original Wagyu draft animal, now government-protected as a tiny native population on the small island of Mishima. These small cattle have fine, curled coats, usually black, but sometimes brown or brindled. The **Japanese Black** is the result of Wagyu being improved for beef over the decades with various European breeds, often different ones in different regions, but including Brown Swiss, Shorthorn, and Devon and to a lesser extent Simmental, Ayrshire, and Holstein. The coat is solid dull black, with a brownish tinge at the hair tips, and the breed has small short horns. The light reddish-brown **Japanese Brown** is from Wagyu improved for beef by the use of Simmental (especially for the larger light-brown Kumamoto strain) and Korean cattle (especially for the reddish-brown Kochi strain) and a bit of Devon. There is also a black **Japanese Poll**, with the polling factor introduced by Aberdeen-Angus, and a **Japanese Shorthorn**, improved with both Dairy and Beef Shorthorn and a touch of Devon and Ayrshire.

The dull black coat of this Wagyu bull, with a hint of brown on the hair tips, comes from its Japanese Black ancestor. *John Goggins*

Welsh Black

In Wales, cattle go back to Celtic times. In later
centuries, Wales was a well-known source of steers
that were driven on foot into the English midlands
to be fattened by graziers for the city beef markets.

Type: taurine
Uses: beef, suckler cow
Coat: black
Horns: middle length

Welsh cows were also traditionally managed and hand-milked by women, who made
sure that their animals were good-tempered as well as good yielders. Thus there is a long
tradition in Wales for both beef and dairy cattle and, in particular, for combining the
two in good suckler cows. The Welsh Black is the result: a dual-purpose breed, valued
especially as a suckler cow in beef herds. It evolved from a combination of local types
such as the handsome Glamorgan (red to mahogany or black, with white markings, including a white finchback and underline); the Montgomeryshire (red shading to smoky
black on face and tail); the short-legged, heavy Anglesey of the Welsh mountains in the
north; and the taller, longer, and more dairy-type Pembroke of the south. The first Welsh
Black breed society was formed in 1873 and re-formed in 1904 to combine the north
and south types into one dual-purpose black breed, preferably a deep dark chocolate
brown-black. There is also a **Polled Welsh Black**.

The original Welsh cattle showed a wide range of coat colors, including bright orange-
red, yellow dun, blue, and mouse as well as the usual solid colors. They also displayed many
patterns: pied, brindled, belted, lineback, and color-pointed. These variations still occur
in what are now described as the **Coloured Welsh** (or "Ancient Cattle of Wales"). There
is also a recognized **White Welsh**, which is white with black points.

The original
Welsh Black
suckler cow
had a fine pair
of middle-
length horns,
rarely seen
today. *Welsh
Black Cattle
Society*

White Park

There is considerable confusion about the **Ancient White Park** and the **American White Park**, but both are based on old British breeds. In Britain, the **White Park** is something rather special. It is an ancient color-pointed breed with longish horns that was generally kept by landed gentry to decorate the parkland on their large estates, and the breed's ancestry comprises what were originally several private herds in England, Scotland, and Wales, each with a distinctive type (Cadzow in Lanarkshire, Chartley in Staffordshire, Dynevor and Vaynol in Wales, and the even more distinctive semi-feral Chillingham in Northumberland). The handsome White Park became the symbol used by Britain's Rare Breeds Survival Trust. There is also a naturally polled breed called the **British White**; this animal, too, is color-pointed, and for many years was assumed to be a polled variety of the White Park, though this belief has since been disproved. And that is where the confusion lies. The story is told in detail in Janet Vorwald Dohner's massive book, *The Encyclopedia of Historic and Endangered Livestock and Poultry Breeds* (2001), but the situation remains a little cloudy.

In 1938, with a new world war on the horizon, some White Park (or, some say, British White) cattle were exported from England to Riverdale Zoo in Toronto; they

In Britain, the White Park has middle-length horns and the direction in which they grow is a fair indication of the old landed-gentry herd from which they originated. In this cow, the horns suggest the Dynevor type from southwest Wales. *Jerome Whittingham, Shutterstock*

were probably from the Cadzow herd. From there in 1941 a pair went to the National Zoo in Washington, D.C., and another pair went to New York's Bronx Zoo and thereafter to the King Ranch in Texas. Also in 1941, because of the war, the British government sent five British White cows and a bull to a state prison farm in Pennsylvania for safekeeping of the breed; here they remained for eight or nine years and then were all sold to a local farmer and from him to a farmer in Illinois, who maintained the herd, with occasional sales of individual animals to neighbors and with a bit of crossing with Angus and Hereford. In 1973, most of this herd was sold to Everett Vannorsdel of Iowa, who also ranched them in Missouri. Vannorsdel set up a White Park Cattle Association of America in 1975, which accepted any white bull or cow having black or red points (regardless of breeding), and registered three or four hundred animals in its herdbook in the first six months. Although some people called these cattle Polled White Park, in actuality the animals were mostly polled British White rather than true White Park, though there may have been White Park in some. Further pure British White cattle were imported from Canada and Britain from 1976 onward, and the breed spread into many states. In the United States, it developed into a heavier and beefier animal than in Britain, though the latter is quickly catching up now that British breeders are concentrating on beef (it was originally dual-purpose).

Meanwhile, after several decades, the horned White Park cattle on the King Ranch were dispersed and purchased in 1981 by the Moeckley family in Iowa, who were already breeding British White and wanted to upgrade. They discovered that at least half of the so-called White Parks from the King Ranch had clearly been crossed with Texas Longhorn, and these they sold off to Longhorn ranches. They used most of the remainder for crossbreeding with their British White bull, but realizing that the White Park was rare, they imported a Cadzow bull in 1987. Other breeders bought the Moeckleys' White Park cows and heifers, and the breed began to spread with the help of artificial insemination of semen from a Dynevor and a Chartley bull. The Moeckleys set up their own registry for White Park cattle and, to avoid confusion with the existing herdbook for the British White in the United States, they named their organization the Horned White Park Cattle Association. The new breeders who had acquired Moeckley stock later reorganized this body into the Ancient White Park Cattle Society of North America. Animals in this register should really be called simply White Park, but some of the polled British White breeders continued to use the name "White Park" or "Polled White Park" for their own cattle, though a new British White Cattle Association of America has now been established.

Whatever the histories and names, the British White in North America is an eye-catching polled breed with its white coat and black or red ears and muzzle. It is not what the British would understand as a White Park. The ancient White Park has always had dramatic horns, though because of similarities in color there was interbreeding in the past from time to time, and for many years even in Britain it was assumed that the British White was no more than a polled variety of the White Park. In the late nineteenth century, it was often called the White Polled. However, in Britain, it was formally acknowledged that they were separate breeds in 1946, when the polled breed officially became the British White. In fact it has been shown that the British White is no more closely related to the White Park than are other British breeds.

The Ancient White Park in the United States is listed by the ALBC as "Critical."

A very special horned white color-pointed herd lives in the northern English county of Northumberland. The **Chillingham** herd has been enclosed in Chillingham Park since at least the seventeenth century (possibly back to the thirteenth). Semiferal, the herd is left to its own devices apart from occasional culling and occasional supplementary hay in winter. The animals are small compared with the White Park (whether British or American), with shaggy white coats, red ears and points, and upright horns, often lyre-shaped in the cows and different from the original White Park herds that have long spreading and curving horns in various forms according to their geographical origins.

The lack of horns in the American White Park suggests that it is in fact a polled British White rather than an Ancient White Park.

Type: taurine
Uses: beef, suckler cow, ornamental
Coat: white over pigmented skin, with black points (occasionally red or dark brown), sometimes colored freckling on shoulders, head, and body (increasingly with crossbreeding).
Horns: long and curving in Ancient White Park; usually polled in American White Park (British White)

Yak

The wild yak is neither *Bos taurus* (humpless taurine cattle) nor *Bos indicus* (humped zebu cattle) but is in a family of its own as *Bos (Poëphagus) mutus*. It is a native of high altitudes in north-central Tibet and is, as *mutus* implies, usually a silent animal apart from a very occasional grunt. It is now rare in the wild.

The domesticated yak is classified as *Bos (Poëphagus) grunniens*. Its homeland is on the Tibetan Plateau, the Himalayas, and Mongolia, and the yak is a shaggy beast suited to the harsh climate of those regions. Its coat is usually black or brown, but there is quite a variety in the domesticant, including white, gray, blue roan, and even pied. It has been domesticated for several thousand years and local types have been developed. An immensely useful animal, the yak gives milk (with a very high level of butterfat, which is used as lighting fuel as well as food), meat, hair for felt to make tents and clothes, skins, dung (for fires as well as manure), and muscle power, especially as a pack animal; it can also pull a plow and be ridden. It is smaller than its surprisingly large wild ancestor. Some are horned and some are polled.

The **Yakow** or *dzo* is the name given to any cross between yak and domesticated cattle, and there is a whole glossary of names for different crosses.

Domesticated yak were first imported into the United States in 1909 but did not have commercial success at the time. More recently, they have been brought into North America as a novelty animal and have also been crossed with cattle (the **Yakmac**, invented in England as a possible hardy upland breed, is a cross with a Highland bull) and with the American bison. The female offspring from crosses with cattle appear to be fertile, though males are sterile. In the bison cross, the yak conformation and coat are dominant in the offspring and the hybrid females have low fertility. Experiments continue in various parts of the world, including three-way crosses involving American bison, yak, and mithun (the handsome white-stockinged domesticated gaur) or bison, yak, and banteng.

> **Type:** yak
> **Uses:** dairy, meat, draft, hair/underwool
> **Coat:** usually black or rusty brown, also various other colors (including all-white) and patterns; shaggy; tail also abundantly hairy from root to tip
> **Horns:** short to middle length; sometimes polled

Opposite, bottom: The rare, wild Tibetan yak generally has a heavy dark brown to black coat, but there is a wide range of colors and patterns in domesticated yak—including the black-and-white effect seen here on the Tibetan Plateau. The scarlet tassels in the ears are, of course, decorations. *Grigory Kubatyan, Shutterstock*

The shaggy coat of the yak covers the full length of the tail and protects the animal from the extreme climate. The hair is a valuable commodity in its mountainous Asian homeland. *Petrov Andrey, Shutterstock*

Appendix

Resources

American Cowman
  http://americancowman.com

American Livestock Breeds Conservancy
  PO Box 477
  Pittsboro, NC 27312
  www.albc-usa.org

Domestic Animal Diversity Information
    System
  http://dad.fao.org

Hoard's Dairyman
  PO Box 801
  Fort Atkinson, WI 53538
  www.hoards.com

National Association of Animal Breeders
  PO Box 1033
  Columbia, MO 65205
  http://naab-css.org

Oklahoma State University Breeds of
    Livestock
  101 Animal Science Building
  Stillwater, OK 74078
  www.ansi.okstate.edu/breeds

Breed Associations

Amerifax Cattle Association
  PO Box 149
  Hastings, NE 68901

American **Angus** Association
  3201 Frederick Boulevard
  St Joseph, MO 64501
  www.angus.org

Ankole Watusi International Registry
  22484 West 239 Street
  Spring Hill, KS 66083

Aubrac International, Inc.
  PO Box 296
  Oak Creek, CO 80467
  www.aubracusa.com

Ayrshire Breeders Association
  1244 Alton Darby Creek Road, Suite B
  Columbus, OH 43228

Barzona Breeders Association of
    America
  PO Box 631
  Prescott, AZ 83602

Beefmaster Breeders Universal
  6800 Park Ten Boulevard, Suite 290 W.
  San Antonio, TX 78213
  www.beefmasters.org

A herd of Holstein cows meanders home.

American **Belgian Blue** Breeders, Inc.
PO Box 154
Hedrick, IA 52563
www.belgianblue.org

Belted Galloway Society
98 Edison Creek Road
Staunton, VA 24001
www.beltie.org

American **Blonde d'Aquitaine**
Association
7407 VZ County Road 1507
Grand Saline, TX 75140
www.blondecattle.org

United **Braford** Breeders
422 E. Main Street, Suite 218
Nacogdoches, TX 75961
www.brafords.org

American **Brahman** Breeders
Association
3003 South Loop West, Suite 140,
Houston, TX 77054
www.brahman.org

International **Brangus** Breeder
Association
PO Box 696020
San Antonio, TX 78269
www.int-brangus.org

Braunvieh Association of America
3815 Touzalin Avenue, Suite 103
Lincoln, NE 68507
www.braunvieh.org

British White Cattle Association of
America
PO Box 281
Bells, TX 75414

American **British White Park**
Association
PO Box 176
Gustine, TX 76455

Brown Swiss Cattle Breeders Association
of America
800 Pleasant Street
Beloit, WI 53511
www.brownswissusa.com

BueLingo Cattle Society
6507 South Highway 215
Charleston, AR 72933
www.buelingo.com

Société des Éleveurs de Bovins **Canadiens**
4865 Boulevard Laurier Ouest
Sainte-Hyacinthe, Quebec, Canada J2S
3V4

American-International **Charolais**
Association
PO Box 20247
Kansas City, MO 64195
www.charolaisusa.com

American **Chianina** Association
PO Box 890
Platte City, MO 64079
www.chicattle.org

North American **Corriente** Association
PO Box 12359
North Kansas City, MO 64116
www.corrientecattle.org

American **Devon** Cattle Association
11035 Waverly
Olathe, KS 66061
www.americandevon.com

American **Dexter** Cattle Association
4150 Merino Avenue
Watertown, MN 55388
www.dextercattle.org

Dutch Belt Cattle Association of
America
c/o American Livestock Breeds
Conservancy
PO Box 477
Pittsboro, NC 27312
www.dutchbelted.com

American **Galloway** Breeders
Association
310 West Spruce
Missoula, MT 59802
www.americangalloway.com

American **Gelbvieh** Association
10900 Dover Street
Westminster, CO 80021
www.gelbvieh.org

American **Guernsey** Association
7614 Slate Ridge Boulevard
PO Box 666
Reynoldsburg, OH 43068

American **Hereford** Association
PO Box 014059
Kansas City, MO 64101
www.hereford.org

American **Highland** Cattle Association
200 Livestock Exchange Building
Denver, CO 80216
www.highlandcattle.org

Holstein Association
1 Holstein Place
Brattleboro, VT 05302
www.holsteinusa.com

American **Jersey** Cattle Association
64846 East Street
Reynoldsburg, OH 43068
www.usjersey.com

North American **Limousin** Foundation
PO Box 4467
Englewood, CO 80155
www.nalf.org

American **Maine-Anjou** Association
PO Box 1100
Platte City, MO 64079
www.maine-anjou.org

American International **Marchigiana**
Society
PO Box 198
Walton, KS 67151
www.marchigiana.org

American **Milking Devon** Association
135 Old Bay Road
New Durham, NH 03855
www.milkingdevons.org

American **Milking Shorthorn** Society
PO Box 449
Beloit, WI 53512

American **Murray Grey** Association
PO Box 60748
Reno, NV 89506
www.murraygreybeefcattle.com

Parthenais Cattle Breeders Association
of America
PO Box 550
Bells, TX 75414

Piedmontese Association of the
United States
343 Barrett Road
Elsberry, MO 63343
www.pauscattle.org

Pineywoods Cattle Registry and
Breeders Association
2262 Highway 59
Spruce Pine, AL 35585

American **Pinzgauer** Association
PO Box 147
Bethany, MO 64424
www.pinzgauers.org

American **Red Poll** Association
PO Box 147
Bethany, MO 68424
www.redpollusa.org

American **Romagnola** Association
3815 Touzalin, Suite 104
Lincoln, NE 68507
www.americanromagnola.com

American **Salers** Association
19590 E. Mainstreet # 202
Parker, CO 80138
www.salersusa.org

Santa Gertrudis Breeders
International
PO Box 1257
Kingsville, TX 78263
www.santagertrudis.com

American **Senepol** Association
PO Box 808
Staham, GA 30606
www.senepolcattle.com

American **Shorthorn** Association
8288 Hascall Street
Omaha, NB 68124
www.shorthorn.org

American **Simmental** Association
1 Simmental Way
Bozeman, MT 59715
www.simmental.org

North American **South Devon**
Association
19590 E. Main Street, Suite 202
Parker, CO 80138
www.southdevon.com

American **Tarentaise** Association
PO Box 34705
North Kansas City, MO 64116
www.usa-tarentaise.com

Texas Longhorn Breeders Association
of America
PO Box 4430
Fort Worth, TX 76164
www.tlbaa.org

North American **Tuli** Association
10853 Forest Drive
College Station, TX 77845
www.tuliassociation.com

American **Wagyu** Association
PO Box 547
Pullman, WA 99163
www.wagyu.org

World **Watusi** Association
PO Box 14
Crawford, NE 69339

White Park Cattle International
c/o Lawrence Alderson (President)
6 Harnage
Shrewsbury, Shropshire SY5 6EJ
United Kingdom

International **Yak** Association
Harris Ridge Road
Kooskia, ID 83539

An Ayrshire cow is intent on meeting the photographer.

An Ankole cow has massive horns and a small sanga hump.

Bibliography

Alderson, Lawrence, and Valerie Porter. *Saving the Breeds: A History of the Rare Breeds Survival Trust.* Robertsbridge, UK: Pica Press, 1994.

Chiperzak, J. *Raising Rare Breeds: Livestock and Poultry Conservation.* Ontario: Joywind Farm Rare Breeds Conservancy Inc., 1994.

Christman, C. J., D. P. Sponenberg, and D. E. Bixby, eds. *A Rare Breeds Album of America Livestock.* Pittsboro, NC: American Livestock Breeds Conservancy, 1997.

Felius, Marleen. *Cattle Breeds: An Encyclopedia.* The Netherlands: Misset, 1995.

Goodwin, Frank. *Life on the King Ranch.* New York: Thomas Y. Crowell Company, 1951.

Li, C., and G. Wiener, eds. *The Yak.* Bangkok: Food and Agriculture Organization–Regional Office for Asia and Pacific.

Payne, W. J. A., and J. Hodges. *Tropical Cattle: Origins, Breeds and Breeding Policies.* Oxford, UK: Blackwell Science, 1997.

Porter, Valerie. *Practical Rare Breeds.* London: Pelham, 1987.

——. *Cows for the Smallholder.* London: Pelham, 1988.

——. *Caring for Cows.* London: Whittet Books, 1991.

——. *British Cattle.* Princes Risborough, UK: Shire Publications, 2001.

——. *Cattle: A Handbook to the Breeds of the World.* Marlborough, UK: Crowood Press, 2007.

——. *Mason's World Dictionary of Livestock Breeds, Types and Varieties, 5th edition.* Wallingford, UK: CABI Publishing, 2002.

Rouse, John E. *World Cattle, III: Cattle of North America.* Norman: University of Oklahoma Press, 1973.

——. *The Criollo: Spanish Cattle in the Americas.* Norman: University of Oklahoma Press, 1977.

Scherf, Beate D., ed. *World Watch List for Domestic Animal Diversity, 3rd edition.* Rome: Food and Agriculture Organization, 2000.

Vorwald Dohner, Janet. *The Encyclopedia of Historic and Endangered Livestock and Poultry Breeds.* New Haven, CT: Yale University Press, 2001.

Wood-Roberts, John. *Shorthorns in the 20th Century UK and Ireland.* Stowmarket, UK: Whittet Books, 2005.

Index

About the Author

Valerie Porter is the editor of *Mason's World Dictionary of Livestock Breeds* and the author of *Cattle: A Handbook to the Breeds of World*, *Caring for Cows*, *Cows for Smallholders*, *Keeping a Cow*, and *British Cattle*, as well as books on chickens, pigs, goats, and sheep. She lives in Milland, West Sussex, in the United Kingdom.

Midhurst and Petworth Observer

About the Photographer

Lynn M. Stone is a nature photographer whose images have appeared in *The Complete Cow* as well as numerous magazines, including *National Geographic*, *Audubon*, *Field and Stream*, and *Ranger Rick*. He lives in St. Charles, Illinois.

Bryant Boyd